Discovering Your Soul's Path

8 Cases of Past Life Regressions Plus Astrological Charts and Psychic Readings

Lee Mitchell

Discovering Your Soul's Path

8 Cases of
Past Life Regressions
Plus Astrological Charts
and Psychic Readings

Copyright © 2018 by Lee Mitchell

ISBN: 978-0-9889250-21

All rights reserved. No part of this publication may be reproduced or utilized in any form or by any means, electronic or mechanical, including photocopying, recording, or by any information storage and retrieval system, without prior written permission from the publisher.

Printed in the United States of America
by Casey Publishing
Highlands Ranch, CO 80126

First Edition

Black Panther

All Big Cats are Guides for Me

When the black panther enters your life as a totem, it awakens the inner passions. This can manifest in unbridled expressions of baser powers and instincts. It can also reflect an awakening of the kundalini, signaling a time of not just coming into one's own power. More so, the keynote of the black panther is Reclaiming One's True Power.

Animal-Speak, The Spiritual & Magical Powers of Creatures Great & Small
Ted Andrews

Table of Contents

Acknowledgments	vii
Introduction to Book Three	1-6
Chapter One: Maggie Bowles, The Caring Pisces Nurse	7-24
Chapter Two: Susan Wilson, Spirit Guides Helping to Light the Way	25-40
Chapter Three: Betty Wessling, The Sales Coach Learning to Receive	41-57
Chapter Four: Martha Shaffer, The Crusader and Teacher	59-75
Chapter Five: Lee Mitchell, The Hypnotherapist	77-95
Chapter Six: Dan Ely, The Compassionate Finance Manager	97-114
Chapter Seven: Priscilla Daniel, The Healer Among Us	115-132
Chapter Eight: Mike Daniel, The Family Man	133-149
Epilogue	151-153
Astrology 101	155-161
Tarot Cards 101	163-169
About the Author	171

Acknowledgements

I want to thank the friends and professionals that helped me complete this most unique book. The book took over a year to complete. Thanks so much to the seven clients plus myself for these eight wonderfully insightful studies of how tools like past life regression, astrology, and tarot readings can help understand our soul's path.

Thank you so much, Marta Shoman, for editing the content of the book. You simplified my ramblings so many times. Your good common sense on wording always came through. Thank you, Maryann Sperry, for your most professional book formatting and cover. Although the idea for the cover was brought to light by my friend, Heather Snowmoon, Maryann was able to produce a marvelous cover that expressed what I was trying to say beautifully.

Thank you so much, Gail Nelson, for you ebook formatting in all its forms. Not only Kindle, but in Smashwords as well. You are so responsive to the call and do it so well. You are a pro.

Finally, I want to thank the thousands of cases over the years who have taught me to ask the right questions in the regression sessions. You have taught me so much that would have been impossible without your kind generosity of your time.

Spirit Guides, Aranthia, Johnathan, Marcy, Simon, Loneagle, Mary-Margaret, Filamenta, and Granny, you are my rock and I could do none of this without your light and strength. Archangels Michael, Raphael, Uriel, and Gabriel, please continue to be with me and show me the way to best be of service.

Love to all my furry babies in spirit: Casey, Nikia, Tasha, Frazier, Dax, Allie, Zebe, and Mikey.

Introduction

The majority of my clients that come for a past life regression or a between lives regression session have a sense of what they are alive to do in this present time. They have a "feel" for their life's purpose. Many know they are light workers and are here to hold the light for us all. Many are from another realm, such as the Fairy realm or advanced societies from another galaxy or planet. Many others simply feel alone and out-of-place being on earth. Many people have traumas that they have suffered from the hands of souls in their soul group. What we are all searching for is confirmation of our assignment on Earth this time. Many I work with, also, want confirmation of their connections to powers from advanced societies. And, in addition, many want confirmation of traumas that they suffer from today so that they may release their emotions around the traumas, move forward, and progress as souls.

This book is based on a multi-faceted approach that I use with people to bring about healing, deeper insight, growth and kindness to oneself.

The Work that Called

Many people ask me how I got interested in hypnotherapy. It is a subject I have been fascinated with all my adult life. When I was 17, I was an avid reader of the books of Edgar Cayce. He was known as the "Sleeping Prophet". He could "see" past lives of his clients. He was a profound herbal and energy healer as well. I remember having a motorcycle accident at 17 and using one of his remedies for scars. Edgar had an international reputation and was known to move into a trance to answer his client's questions when they called on the phone. As a teenager reading his books, the past life information he gave to others was intriguing for me.

In my twenties, I read Jane Roberts's book, "Seth Speaks" which was first published in 1972 and is still in print. Seth, an advanced being in spirit, actually channeled through Jane and spoke of knowledge concerning the effect of past lives on our current lives. I graduated from college at 21 with a growing curiosity and interest in what these spiritual intuitives could tell us about past lives.

In 1988, "Many Lives, Many Masters" became a best seller written by Dr. Brian Weiss. This book brought an increased awareness in past life work to the public and sparked an interest in people seeking past life regression work.

When Dr. Michael Newton released his books, "Journey of Souls" in 1994 and "Destiny of Souls" in 2000, I resonated with his process of hypnotherapy and especially his creation of the "Life Between Lives" sessions he describes in these books. The sessions discussed in "The Life Between Lives" involved clients entering the deeper mental states of Theta brain waves which are accessed through deep relaxation techniques.

In 2008, I completed my certification as a Past Life Regression Therapist with a colleague of Dr. Michael Newton. I now perform past life as well as between life regression sessions. My Denver-based practice serves people from across the US and Canada as the public's understanding of how past lives shape one's present situation continues to grow.

My website, www.crystalsoulpath.com, gets requests to book a scheduled session for many personal reasons. I tell people my work is like reading a mystery novel every day. I never know where the client is going to take us and where we will eventually land. All of this information comes from the client in an altered state while they access their subconscious mind. I have discovered from thousands of case studies that many people can change forever in their present life by returning to an important past life. When this occurs, the process of engaging with an important event or relationship in the past life allows their higher self to process the event from a higher perspective that when they actually experienced it in the past life. The session frees them to more fully step into their soul's path in this current life by releasing any remaining emotion they may have had around the traumatic event.

Integrating the Modalities: Regression Sessions, Natal Astrology Interpretation, Psychic Tarot Readings

This body of work is going to be quite different than my previous two books, "The Soul's Journey" and "The Soul's Divine River of Life." In the earlier books, I related my most intriguing cases of past life regression and between lives regression. Cases of parallel lives, past lives from other planets and galaxies, and past lives from Atlantis were just a few of the topics we discussed. Clients even experienced past lives in the Fairy realm.

As I have practiced and taught astrology for the past thirty years, I have learned to glean the information from a client's astrological natal chart and add it to a client's information about why they are here in their current life. The astrological information added to the experience of the past life regression helps the client process and understand what they have come to work on in this life. With this process, their soul's experience grows to a higher dimension of understanding. A higher dimension allows the client from a soul perspective to understand more clearly why they are here and what is their "soul's purpose." A higher dimension allows us to drop the attention to everyday tasks, although we must perform them to be on planet Earth, and focus on the more important tasks of relationships, missions, goals, forgiveness, and even love.

You will be reading about current cases of clients I have worked with who have experienced one or more important past lives with me, but have also stayed to do an Astrological Natal Chart. Some of the clients I have retrieved from my first and second books and asked them to come again and do this wonderful session with me as a follow-up some years later.

Some of the cases are with clients that are fresh and new to the experience as well. This book even includes case studies of my partner, Dan Ely and myself, as well. We, too, want to have a deeper understanding of how our past lives influence our current individual life and committed relationship with each other.

I have changed all the names to protect the client's privacy in each chapter. You may see yourself in many of their situations, and hopefully, this information will influence you to experience a past life regression session and/or an astrology chart interpretation for yourself!

In addition, since I have been performing psychic intuitive readings for over 20 years, I have incorporated psychic reading information for the present to complete the picture for each one of us in the book.

In the case of traumas experienced from past lives, you will learn how I use "attachment releases" to help dissolve these traumas that have carried over into the client's present life. By dissolving the trauma, one is more fully able to tackle the task of their present life, and can once and for all, let go of the baggage of that past life they have been carrying around.

We all want clear understanding of our roles and how to best complete them successfully. Many times clients ask that they want clarity so they can complete what is a very difficult life and return to the magical place in spirit with their loving soul group once more.

I have learned detail ways to explain in a person's Astrological Natal Chart where they have come from in their most recent past life and what they have come to primarily work on in their current life. This information helps the client to not waste time on unimportant tasks and to focus on primarily their mission in this present life. You will discover that this information only confirms what they see and experience in their past life experience.

Wrapping all this up will be the actual psychic reading prediction for the near future to complete the person's clarity on their Path. I will break down the meaning of the tarot cards and how it is so appropriately relating to their previous information about their soul's purpose. My Spirit Guides also come through in the readings to add more detail in answering the client's questions about their future.

For additional help, I have included "Astrology 101" and "Tarot Cards 101" chapters at the end of the book for references as you read the book. Be sure to check these out!

Join me for the experiences, so that you too, may understand how to use these tools to understand your reason for being on the planet today!

Lee Mitchell
Certified Past Life Regression Therapist
January, 2018

Chapter One

Maggie Bowles
The Caring Pisces Nurse

In our current life, our soul's path often brings us to face the "baggage" from past lives. This was the case with Maggie Bowles, a Registered Nurse with a Master's degree in Management who I had worked with for several years. I knew her to be highly intelligent as well as a caring Mother to two teenage daughters. I, also, was aware that her tumultuous relationship with Bobby, a long-time significant other, was a source of pain and unresolved feelings that did not support her growth.

I was drawn to help her unpack the obstacles that limited her growth through past life regression therapy and astrological counseling. Our ability to look at her past lives would provide clues to why she felt she must stay in the relationship with Brian, no matter what the consequences were to her. Examining her natal astrology chart offers additional insight to her strong personality and her emotionally driven connection to Brian.

Maggie historically had an almost fanatical need to be with Bobby, despite his short temper and his poor treatment of her. These were signs that I had learned to recognize that some trauma between them from a past life might be causing her need to stay with Bobby above all else. His behavior, in time, also caused her daughters to dislike him. Despite this, from prior tarot card readings I had had with Maggie, I saw that Bobby admired all of Maggie's achievements.

Over the years, Bobby changed his career from construction to education and earned a teaching degree in his 40s. This professional shift caused him to feel better about himself. I had hoped it would also help him treat Maggie with more care than in the past.

But Bobby severed the relationship late in 2016 in anger and with the ultimatum that he needed time apart from Maggie. I hoped that by bringing her into my book as one of the cases, we could get to the real reason Maggie clung to the hopes that one day Bobby would change and treat her much more compassionately.

So in January of 2017, as I inducted Maggie into a slightly altered state using hypnotherapy, she saw herself as a little boy of 7 years old in brown leather tunic and shorts with white tights. His name was Daniel, Maggie told me. Daniel was standing in a castle that was not his home and was in some other country, she told me. It was Persia and he was an orphan, she finally revealed to me. She said Daniel felt very cold and alone there. The year was 1792.

The next scene Maggie saw Daniel at the age of 20. He was looking at a guillotine. He was standing next to the person that pulls the guillotine on the prisoner. This man did not like what he had to do, Maggie told me. He was a peasant and was told to do this terrible job. Next, Maggie, as "Daniel", saw that the prisoner was the soul essence of Bobby and was brought forward to be punished. He was going to be killed by the guillotine. He robbed some business. He did it to stay alive, she told me. He was robbing to feed Daniel as well. He was Daniel's closest friend and he was robbing for food for both of them. Daniel feels guilty because his friend got caught and was having to pay for his misdeeds.

Maggie goes on to explain that Daniel knew that his friend did it for him. They needed money and food. Daniel was in a state of poor health as he watched his friend die at the guillotine. Daniel had been so sick that he was near death when his friend had stolen food for both of them. I asked if Daniel's friend was older, and Maggie said yes. His friend was between 35 and 40 years old.

Maggie went on to say that she saw that Daniel grew up on the streets. His friend took him in. His friend was a carpenter and a blacksmith. She told me that the two souls have been together in lives before. When I asked her what she was seeing, she told me that she could feel that they loved each other, these two men. She and the soul of Bobby have loved each other in many lives, no matter what the relationship had been. All of this information was being sensed from her higher self as she saw the scene unfold.

Maggie told me Daniel went on to live a very lonely life. He died at 68, never getting over losing his best friend. He felt so sad that last day of his life, she said. Maggie said that, today, she still gets that sad, sad feeling when she thinks of Bobby in her current life. When Daniel dies, she saw that the soul of Bobby met Daniel's soul to take him to his spiritual home in the spirit realm.

In putting closure to that life, Maggie saw that the man performing the death with the guillotine is her brother in her current life. I asked her to ask her higher self about her soul's purpose in coming into that life as the little orphan boy. Maggie answered that she was to experience love. She emotionally felt that love that day, during the session we were having, that the friend had had for the poor boy, Daniel. I have discovered that the goal of "feeling love" is a common theme for souls to learn, and many times it is derived through pain and loss in their relationships on earth.

As Maggie ventured into her second past life, she saw herself outside in a meadow. She felt it was a tropical climate. Then she saw herself walking on a beach with lots of rocks. I asked her to describe her dress. She was a young girl of 16 who was barefoot and wearing a burlap dress. Maggie says her name was "Surmara" and that she was of Hawaiian or Polynesian descent on an island in the Pacific in the year 1942.

I asked Maggie to ask her higher self if this was her most recent past life and she answered that it was not. I immediately knew the life would not be a long one. Next, very suddenly, she sees that she slipped and fell on the rocks on the beach and drowned in the ocean! It was an accident, she said.

I asked her to tell me why she left so early in that life. Maggie replied that she wasn't going down the right path as Surmara. I believe that we all choose when we leave a life, whether it's through an illness or an accident. Our higher self knows when it is time to leave our present life for a number of reasons. Maggie went on to say that something was about to happen to her family in the village. She saw that they were to be robbed and killed by another village group who wanted to steal from them and take all they had. She, as a soul, had planned to be away. She did not want to die a painful death. Maggie said that as that 16 year old girl, she was very happy. She was living a wonderful life as a teenager on a beautiful island. I ask her to identify the robbers. She did not recognize their soul essences. Maggie recognized Bobby as her brother in that life. Her daughter, Annie, was her mother and her current brother was her father in this past life on the beautiful island. There was even a friend visiting her parents in the tiny village that was killed as well. Maggie sensed the friend as the soul of her present father in her current life.

When I asked about her soul's purpose in that life, Maggie heard from her higher self that it was to learn youth and to simply learn how to think as a child again. She did accomplish that and was ready to go when she drowned.

As we pulled through the energy of Maggie's master guide, she remembered him from a session we had years ago. His name is George. When we asked him if he was her master guide in these two previous lives, he told Maggie that he had always been her master guide. He looked to be in his 60s with grey hair and mustache, she said. He felt strong, compassionate, yet stern, to her.

George went on to tell her that she had had many lives on earth and twenty-two of them had been with Bobby. I asked George, her master guide, to explain Bobby and Maggie's soul contract in this life. He told her that they both came in with many challenges for each of them to overcome in order to be together. When you make a soul contract between two souls, it's for both of you to grow as souls by helping each other learn things you both need for your soul's growth.

George went on to say that Maggie was to use this time alone now to work on herself. Her self-doubt and insecurity were holding her back and keeping her from moving this relationship forward. Until those changes could improve, Bobby would not be there for her. George said that her feeling that she "was never good enough" was holding her back in this life. He went on to say that Bobby really did love her and that he would always be her true love.

Maggie also felt a second guide named Delita. She was the energy of a "Tinkerbell," Maggie said. These were the only two guides that came through that day. Many times the master guide wants to be the main connection of the past life experience so that the message can be very clear why the client just saw the particular lives they saw.

George went on to say that the two particular lives that Maggie experienced where to reassure her that she and Bobby have been together before, and that they will always come back together in lives over their many lifetimes together.

What George said had been the missing piece I was looking for. The obsession the Maggie had about Bobby was explained. They had come back with a contract to be together, but not before some significant lessons were learned by both of them. George went on to tell Maggie that nothing in this life was to be easy. She asked for hard lessons. Even her job was to be challenging. But he said, get ready, all the things in her life were about to change this year for the better. She would be traveling eventually. He said "I see light for you".

In ending, George advised Maggie to give Bobby time. He takes longer than you to process things in his mind. He can't give you what you need right now. He denies that he is trying to change, but he really is trying. George told Maggie to leave Bobby to his time alone. He needs this time alone to process a great deal.

Months went by, and I would occasionally do a tarot card reading for Maggie. We were seeing that a job opportunity was coming to her that might include some traveling. Something she had always wanted to do. So in June of 2017, after no connection to Bobby for over six months, and the job situation having not shifted, I asked Maggie to participate in a second regression session in which I just asked for her guides to come through and talk to her. I was getting ready to start this book and she was to be the first chapter. She readily agreed, although a little apprehensive.

As I inducted Maggie into an altered state, she saw an outside scene with many beautiful flowers. Next, she saw a bench. An angel is sitting on the bench. Maggie says she knows this angel. It is George, her master guide. He begins to speak to her...

"Maggie needs to try harder. We have given her so many gifts and she is not using them. She is spinning. She is not moving forward. What is holding you back?"

I ask her to explain what George meant by this message. She said that her gifts were her two beautiful daughters, being born with a good brain, having the ability to be kind toward others in her work life, a very loving person to those she cared about, and a jest for fun in life. The fact that she is not moving forward is not so much the guilt she felt from the past life of not being able to help Bobby when he suffered so in being killed in the guillotine, but that she is so sad that they are not together already. She wanted for them to be together forever in this present life. She is just too committed to Bobby in hopes that the outcome would be what she wanted.

I believe Maggie was not prepared, as a soul, for the challenges that she put upon herself in this life, and wanted a simpler answer to her needs. Her needs were to be with Bobby as soon as possible to share their lives together. Many times in the spirit realm as we decide to incarnate, we set some pretty ambitious goals. Then we come into the human body connected to relationships that we cannot control. We soon realize we may have asked for more than we were prepared to achieve.

George repeated what he had said to her in the earlier session back in January of 2017. She must work on her self-esteem and confidence before Bobby would show up again. George told her that it will be her decision to be with Bobby after she makes these changes. He said she needs a clear head when she meets up with him again.

He went on to tell Maggie to, "Be Happy." Keep going to the gym. Get out more. Go out with her single girlfriends. At this point, Maggie told me she heard the Beyonce song, "All the single ladies", in her head. George said that the loss of confidence and self-esteem was not just from the life as Daniel, but from a series of many past lives that she had experienced. Because of the build-up of these past life experiences, one of

Maggie's goals in this present life as Maggie was to improve her confidence. We will investigate her personality at birth, next, when we look at her astrological natal chart, to see if she came in with the tools to achieve this goal.

George said that when Maggie had worked on these attitudinal changes to achieve more confidence, she would meet someone to date. She would meet them either through work or doing some physical activity. It must be all about changing her energy. He repeated that Maggie could change her perception and be happy. Appreciate what she had in life. He went on to say that her current job wasn't very healthy for her and that it did not help her energy. There would be a new opportunity for a job change coming soon. He said someone would call her. There would be traveling involved later on in the job and that she would be able to sometimes work out of her home. She had been looking for all these features in a career move for quite some time.

In closing, George said that Maggie could have the world if she chose it. Maggie was extremely relieved. Though she was not giving up on reconnecting to Bobby, stepping into a more happy time in her life with the right attitude sounded great to her. Even dating seemed exciting at this time. It was all up to Maggie now. George had given her some clear challenges that she knew she had to accomplish to complete this life and make it the happy one she had envisioned.

After the conversations with George, it was time to look at Maggie's astrological natal chart to see what she did indeed plan to work on in this current life. As you can see from Maggie's natal chart on the following page, Maggie is a Pisces with a

Cancer rising and a Libra moon. I call those three distinctive planets the "Skeleton" of the human soul in this life.

My definition of a "Skeleton" of the soul is that in every Astrology birth chart there are three major forces that are the foundation of a person's life-long exterior and interior worlds. These are the Rising or Ascendant planet found at the time of birth and ruling the cusp of the first house, the Sun which expresses our outer expressions, or our ego, and the Moon which expresses our deeper, internal self.

She is a hard-working, take action Sun personality but with a very sensitive approach to her interaction with others. Pisces are the most intuitive and psychically aware sign of the zodiac. But then she has a Cancer rising sign or ascendant. A rising sign is the "armor" we wear when we go out into the world. Our Sun is our true nature, but we will feel like the rising sign to others we work or interact with during the day. Cancers are also hard working and the caretaker sign of the zodiac. They want to mother us all with their caring, but they are also very sensitive to being hurt by others. Cancers are the crab that will crawl into its shell at the first sign of danger. All Cancers want a retreat home to run to. They may not own their home but they want to know they always have a safe place to go to when fear comes over them. When I asked Maggie about this part of herself, she said her bedroom in her home, which she owns, was her retreat room from the world. She so enjoyed going to her private room to give her quiet time alone.

The third component of Maggie's Astrological Skeleton is her Libra Moon. A Libra Moon is all about balance. Libra signs are masculine in nature and a cardinal sign. They like to take action and solve problems. The Moon is our emotional nature; so Maggie would appear strong and masculine in her emotional nature with the opposite sex. This has always been reflected in the way Bobby feels about her. He feels she is very competent and successful. Maggie has come to give love but certainly wants to receive it as well. She has picked some strong challenges for herself. We all, as souls, pick the time, date and year to be born for all the reasons I mentioned earlier.

Other definitions that need to be described are the three basic modes of energy called Cardinal, Fixed, and Mutable elements. These will determine how each soul responds to life depending on how many of their planets are in each of these energies. Cardinal describes a soul of action. Action people are fast, direct and to the point. Fixed elements describe people who are reticent and non-committal. They are a force that is quiet and organized. They may be stubborn and set on a path at all times. Mutable energies describe people who are pliable and adaptable. They may seem easygoing and free-flowing. Plus, they are centered on the importance of their relationships.

To begin with looking at one's chart for indicators of their most recent past life, we must go to where Saturn is in the chart. We must also look at Saturn's ruler, Capricorn. The location of Saturn in a natal chart has serious implications for someone's soul path. Maggie has Saturn in her eighth house of death, regeneration, other people's money and the deep understanding of psychic facilities. Saturn is where we have suffered in the most recent life. Maggie, in her most recent life, was dependent on other people's money for her survival and livelihood. She was not making the decisions for her life's path. She worked for the group success. She was what we might call somewhat "invisible" in her past life. She, as a soul, wants to change that in her present life.

By having Mercury conjunct Saturn, her communication planet, she learned not to speak her truth. She may have been punished for trying to be seen and heard. Capricorn rules her seventh house. She is coming back in this life to be strong and dependable in all relationships. In her most recent past life, she was unable to be strong, self-reliant, and dependable. Maggie found that she failed others in being available for them. Capricorn is an earth sign and is also a cardinal sign. She will take

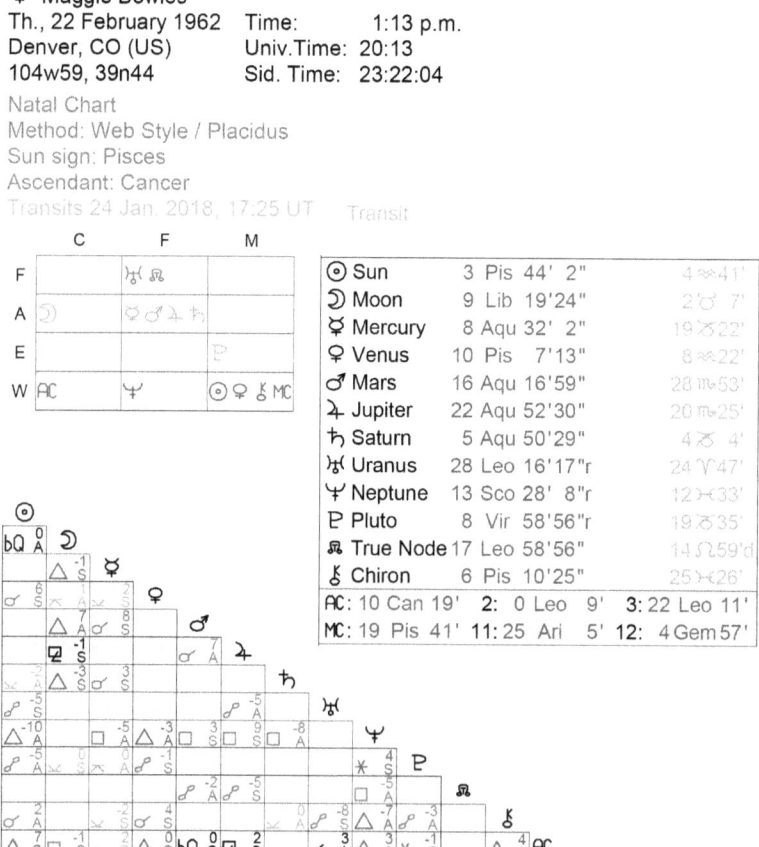

action to work in partnerships in this life. These partnerships might be love partnerships, business partnerships, or family partnerships. Capricorns are the hardest working sign of the zodiac. Maggie will be steadfast in her determination to work hard for her career, her romantic partner, and her daughters, as well. Knowing Maggie as I do, I see that she clearly gives of herself constantly to others.

Another very strong indicator for someone's life path is the North and South nodes of the Moon. Nodes are simply certain degrees in the atmosphere around the moon. They are

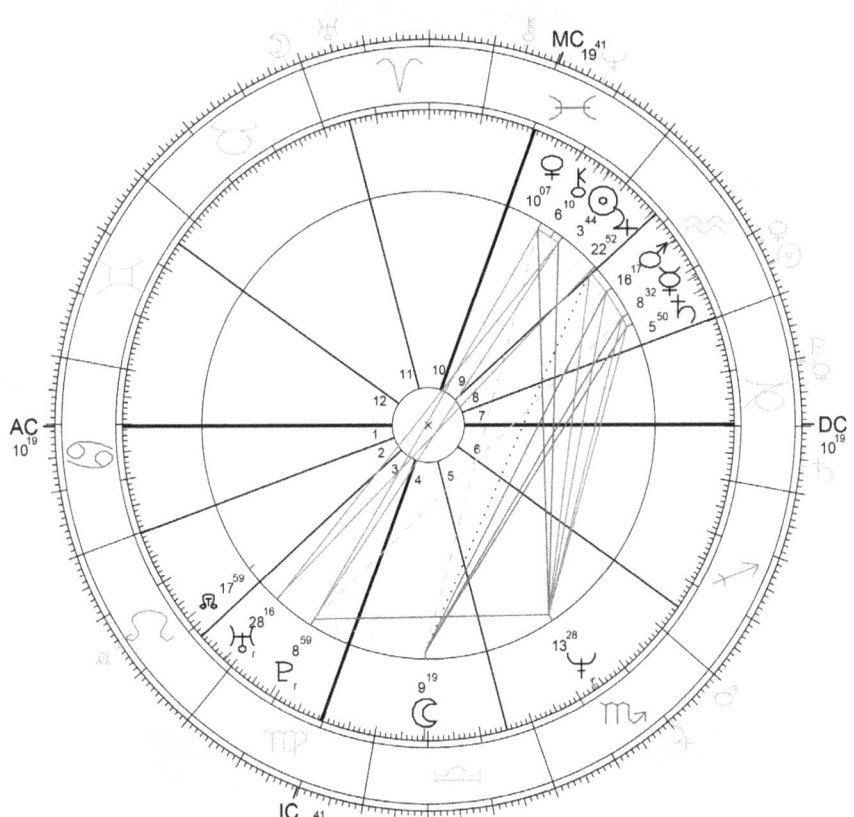

not actually physical objects. They indicate what type of life challenges you have experienced in your most recent life, as indicated by the placement of the South Node, and what you came to work on as life goals in your present life, indicated by the placement of the North Node.

Maggie's North Node is in her second house indicated by the curvy icon in that house. That automatically means her South Node is in the eighth house. It's always in the opposite house of the North Node. That is confirming that Maggie's most recent life came from a life of not being in a position of power over her life. Someone else took care of her needs and gave her food and shelter. By having a house ruled by Leo for her second house where the North Node is located, Maggie wanted to come in being very strong and a true leader. Leos are fire signs and are called the lion of the jungle. They are leaders and want to be looked up to and complimented for their caring deeds. Maggie returned to this life to balance her soul's path by creating an independent lifestyle. In this life she has made the decisions of her life concerning money and material things. The second house rules money and how we look at our possessions. Maggie is a single mother raising two teenage daughters on her own with some help from her ex-husband. Bobby has never offered to help her in any financial way, and she has never asked him to.

The final indicator of a past life experience in the astrological natal chart is the placement of the asteroid Chiron. It is important to know what house it is in and the ruler of that house. Maggie has her Chiron in the 9th house. Chiron is an asteroid that is noted for being "the wounded healer." Maggie's soul might have been working on the soul's healing of the 9th house over many lifetimes. She is highly psychic with her Neptune in her 5th house and trining* Chiron. Many religious leaders, intuitives, and psychics have Neptune in the 5th house. The 9th house is all about higher education, traveling, (Maggie enjoys traveling), and higher consciousness. By having her Sun, Jupiter, Chiron, and Venus all in her 9th house and trining* Neptune, Maggie has come from healing lives, religious lives, and evolved lives where she dealt with the higher consciousness.

Maggie oversees other nursing staff and would be considered a teacher to many in her current job. This would be a ninth house characteristic for sure. But her healing, religious and higher-consciousness skills may have caused her in previous lives to not be considerate of other people and could have caused some of her relationships harm. Therefore, in this life, she needs to reacquaint herself to hardship and pain among her family, friends, and romantic connections.

This allows her to release these old feelings of poor decisions and allow her to free herself to be happy and to love. This is the goal of Chiron, to release and move on to a higher plane for her soul.

All of her planets in the ninth house are ruled by Pisces except for Jupiter which is in Aquarius. Even Aquarius is a very progressive sign and known for its connection to the higher realms of consciousness. Maggie is a soul with much experience and wisdom. In this lifetime she is attempting to pull herself back to center, yet she is not drawing on these abilities as much as she is working on regaining self-confidence. We, as souls, are always trying to keep our growth experiences in balance.

*Trine is an aspect between two planets or asteroids that is 120 degrees apart. This aspect denotes harmony between the two planets and brings benefits to the person.

Maggie's Jupiter opposes* her Uranus. This causes her to be strong willed. She needs to cultivate patience and forethought, for her reflexes are fast and her mind is keen. She will always cater to the unusual and unexpected response when directing someone in training, as any aspect to Uranus brings on the energy of Uranus which is a force that is strong but unexpected and happens when one least expects it to happen.

The fact that seven of Maggie's major planets are in the southern hemisphere, (which is the upper half of the circle), tells me that she will always deal with the public to find her success in life. She will not go back to being "invisible" in her most recent past life. She will be heard in this life!

We see in Maggie a strong soul that says it is time to be happy again in strength and love for others. It is time to feel good about herself before she recalls all her intuitive abilities.

As a soul, Maggie asked for challenges in a love connection with Bobby as well as a loving connection to her daughters. These relationships force her to test her heart connection with other souls. This life is to re-awaken all the love and tenderness that she, as a soul, has had prior to this life.

I discovered that Maggie has a very close connection with her master guide, Angel George. She feels him very clearly and can hear his words in her head better than many I work with. She also has dreams that are many times messages for her. All

*Opposition: *Oppositions are opposing planets at 180 degrees apart that must be reconciled. Oppositions can cause you to be pulled apart by two contrary energy pulls. It forces us to make a choice between the two forces.*

these indicators tell us she is closely connected to the higher dimensions which would be expected from a Sun in Pisces.

After a past life regression and a natal Astrology reading, we worked with the 78 card Tarot card deck to see if the cards could add to our understanding about Maggie's path. I also knew that the Tarot card reading drew upon my own spirit guides as a resource for insight and information beyond what the cards could tell us. As I spread the cards out, I also hear my guides talking to me, showing me images in my head, and making me feel emotions to help better explain the interpretation of the cards.

I did see that in May of 2017, Maggie really jumped on the band wagon to find a new position. The Knight of Wands was coming up in every spread which means new position or new home that the client is changing to in their near future. But over the summer months of June, July, and August, I also saw that there would be frustrations, (the five of Wands), over many of the decisions that the new job would entail. I do see that Maggie stays with the situation hoping it will smooth itself out, indicated by the Judgement card and the Queen of Swords.

Finally, I looked at her relationship with Bobby, and it looked spotty over the spring, summer, and even into the fall. The two cards that kept coming through most often were the five of Cups and the nine of Swords. The five of Cups told me that she was disappointed about her life and what was happening. The nine of Swords told me that she did not want to reach out to Bobby, but instead pull back from connecting to him. She felt that it was his turn to change for this relationship. She had given too much in the past and it had not made her happy, no matter what she did. It was obviously time for her to make changes in her life which would impact her for the rest of her life. These changes would be for her to stand up for her happiness and not give all her love to others.

All these indicators can help one to move forward where they may have been stuck before. Three different disciplines addressing similar themes can help Maggie move forward with the confidence that she is fulfilling the path she came to achieve for her soul's growth.

Maggie is a strong soul that has been lacking in confidence because of the traumatic recent past lives she has chosen. Her present life path is to regain her strength and confidence through challenging career positions and uncomfortable personal relationships that force her to stand up for what she deserves. That is exactly what Maggie is now doing for herself. She is on her way to success.

Chapter Two

Susan Wilson

Spirit Guides Helping to Light the Path

It is my intention to help people understand the unusual paths we pick for ourselves through past life regression. A good case study for this understanding is the second analysis from a session with Susan Wilson who was originally a Denver based client and now resides in Colorado Springs. Susan was in my first book in two separate chapters. Her sessions were so intriguing, I was compelled to bring them to the reader's attention. Now, today, several years later I felt drawn to have another session with Susan concerning her soul's path and the progress she was making in her current life.

Susan and I had many sessions back in 2012. I saw that she was a soul that had been a warrior in past lives and had evolved over lifetimes to take on complex lives and keep evolving. We quickly became friends, and if the truth be told, I believe we have been sisters in a past life.

I invited her to have a session to support her in a crucial shift in her life. Susan had years of experience in software sales.

Both in California and Colorado, she had worked in examining contracts her clients had using technology from Microsoft, Dell, and other programs. Her attention to detail is what had made her so successful. And her kindness with the clients helped her to achieve the sales goals her managers asked her to accomplish. However, the years of long hours were starting to wear on her.

Susan felt it was time for a change. She recognized she was interested in developing new skills. Some of these skills involved metaphysical training and some nutritional training. She picked up the ability to read Tarot cards easily and quickly. She had the amazing ability to see premonitional dreams of events that would eventually become true. Susan, also, had the ability to heal aches and pains of others by the laying on of her hands, similar to Reiki training.

Susan took some time off from work last year and took some courses in nutrition certification classes. Teaching healthy nutrition to others had always been a desire of hers, as well as the interest in spirituality. She was also a wonderful cook. Susan wondered if any of these subjects could start her on a new career path at the age of fifty-two.

I suggested that a past life regression session would help her get a direction. Many times the sessions turn into conversations with the client's guides if that is what is most important for them to experience. Not always are the past lives the most important thing to revisit. I left it up to Susan and her spirit guides to direct us where to go. I am just the facilitator.

As we began the session, Susan quickly slipped into an altered state of consciousness. In January, 2017, at my office in my home in Highlands Ranch, Susan saw swirling colors; purple, yellow, and orange, all around her, as if they were swirling oil on top of water. It felt peaceful to her, she said. Next, she was looking down a hallway that sounded hollow to her. There was no floor below her. She saw bright lights before her and they kept getting brighter and brighter in the hallway. Susan said "I have been here before, but it feels different somehow. I can feel the air. I see big eyes in front of me. It is source. It's so bright. My guides are shielding me from so much bright light being given off."

Next, Susan was shown an empty room to go in to. There were a group of her guides behind her and she could see the purple, yellow, and orange colors again along with the eyes in the room before her. These beings in the room were a different group of beings than the guides she was used to communicating with. Susan said these guides were very wise and powerful. It is possible they were more advanced beings than her immediate spirit guides. Next, she felt a cloak of light coming over her. She could see the colors just flowing from her like a cloak covering her. She saw herself standing with her arms outstretched and looking up.

Now she could feel something on her third eye. Susan wondered if the wise beings were doing something with energy to open her third eye. Instead, she felt they were drawing something out through the area in her forehead. She could feel the energy working right in front of her forehead. She told me she could feel it inside her head in the area where her eyes were. "Knowledge, she heard. They are pulling knowledge I have learned from my past lives. The color hue is blue now, liquid blue all around me", she reported.

Susan then felt small figures around her. She once again saw these figures in color hues. She saw yellow, blue and green shades in front of her. She said they were very close to her. She felt them touching her shoulders! Next, she saw the small beings put something inside of her. "They are not using my third eye. It is light energy of some sort", she said.

The light was very intense and very bright. One being got very close and touched Susan's head. He was expressing to her through telecommunication that the small beings were taking all the sorrow of the world out of her and putting back light energy into her. Susan said her shoulders felt so heavy. They were heavy with the pain of the world. Breathing heavy, she could feel the beings lifting the weight off her shoulders.

I called on Susan's guides to help her see her new path more clearly. Susan was immediately shown a steep mountain. She could only see the left side, and described it as beautiful, very lush and green with wonderful trees. She felt she had the energy to climb it. She said it reminded her of the movie, "Heidi" in the Swiss Alps. Her guides told her it was a long, long journey ahead of her. She was seeing a little girl with a short dress on. Her name was Lillie. She asked her guides if she was to do this journey alone. They told her, "Just go."

Many people are not clear about their path, and Susan was no exception. She asked about a small business she had thought about opening. Her guides responded, "It is not your purpose." Then Susan asked them to show her the new path so that she could understand what she came to accomplish in this part of her life. Most clients I work with realize that they have interests and talents, but they are not clear on how to turn these interests into careers.

The guides showed her that the path opens on the mountain and she sees that the clouds clear about the mountain. They tell her that if she continues to do as she is doing, it will just happen. The guides tell Susan it is about the giving. It is about letting the light come out. Joy, light, hope, and kindness are to be her path. They tell her she is a lightworker. The guides show her walking on the path, going forward. It may seem steep, they tell her, but it is just like walking down a fresh Spring path. She hears pebbles move, birds singing, and small creatures in the grass moving. She sees that the sky is blue. Am I on the right path currently, she asks?

Susan's guides insist that it is important to rest from the crazy world. They tell her that her life is becoming balanced now. (Just recently, coupled with leaving her stressful job, Susan had moved from Steamboat Springs to Colorado Springs and into a quiet neighborhood away from the busy city streets.) They tell her she is letting go of tenseness from others. She said now I can send out light instead of absorbing so much darkness from others.

She tells me she was supposed to absorb the evil and darkness. She cleaned it up for others. Now, they are showing her that she can give light back. She will be transforming, her guides say. The work isn't inside of her, they say. It is now work she will do outside of herself. In the past, she had absorbed the dark energy of others. Now she will spread the light from herself to others outside of herself.

Next, her guides show her the skeleton structure, as if she were in an anatomy class. Am I to teach nutrition, she asks? "If you want", they say. Once again, they show her the steep hill, but now it becomes an easy pathway. It is not what she does, but how she feels about it. Next, she sees an avalanche coming down the mountain, in her mind. The scene is being washed away...

The next scene is of a hat. It goes over Susan's face and buckles at the neck. "We put many hats on. I am learning the hat of wisdom. How we define ourselves is by the hat we wear. We can wear different hats and be successful. Some are too tight and can limit us, she says." Susan says all this to me as she is being shown the hat and its many shapes and sizes.

Once again, for clarification, I asked her guides, is a nutritionist to be Susan's new role? All she was shown was bright purple clouds and then the skies clearing. Purple is the crown chakra color and direct connection to your higher consciousness. The guides want her to make that decision by connecting with her higher self. The best way to do that is through meditation.

We asked that Susan's personal guides join us once again. She knew one as "Bear." He comes in as a big hearted bear with his nose down. Secondly, Eric, her Master Guide, enters and appears as a big old tree. Then we see Owl and Wolf coming through. They are as their names describe. Finally, Dawn enters the scene. She appears as a loving woman wearing a long dress. Susan sees that there is yellow light on her right and green light on her left. Yellow is the color of the third chakra representing strong personal self-esteem and green is the color of the fourth chakra representing the heart and love.

Eric tells Susan that it's time to move forward. He encourages her to believe that things will be taken care of. He shows her a hummingbird which signifies joy and beauty. Next, she sees a live, human heart. We understand that to mean Susan must go forward to find her passion. Find what excites her heart. Eric tells her that she has not experienced enough yet to know what will make her happy.

Surprisingly, Bear tells her that a "bear of a man" is in her future. He is big-hearted. He is strong and powerful, yet comforting. He is showing me with the bear, she says. I am alone but he is energetically with me. He will be a partner. In a couple of years I will meet him. It will happen very casually. He will not do the work with me in any of my endeavors, but he will be my strong wall to lean on. He is a protector with a heart filled with light.

"The guides are showing me meeting him", Susan says. "He just comes to me with a big heart. He has facial hair. He is a burly guy with hair. He enjoys the mountains and the outdoors." Bear, her guide, is putting his big hand on her butt, she says. He says, "Just move. Just go, go, go. Step out in faith," she tells me. "He says goodbye to me", Susan says. "As he leaves, he reaches for my face and kisses me". "My guides are all filled with joy for me", she says.

Susan left the session feeling lighter if not somewhat light-headed. She was ready to trust the guides to show signs of specific doors to walk through in her near future. Susan could feel an inner shift and was prepared to embrace it.

A few weeks later, I prepared Susan's Natal Astrology chart and traveled to her home to discuss it. Attached is the Astrological Natal chart for Susan Wilson. As you can see her skeleton of Sun, Moon and Rising Sign are all in Earth signs. Her sun is in Virgo, her moon is in Capricorn, and she has a rising sign in Taurus. All this makes for one practical, grounded, hard-working gal. As a Virgo, she is a perfectionist. She is her own worst critic. She tells herself she is not hard-working enough, not creating enough sales, not achieving the goals she wants to reach all the time. Many times I would hear later that she exceeded her sales goals, but she never seemed to be happy with the fact that she worked so hard. That is a characteristic of an unevolved Virgo, and Susan is attempting to change that about her soul in this current life.

Having a moon in Capricorn makes her emotional nature very responsible and dependable. The way she would show someone that she cared or loved them would be to make them a nice dinner, clean their clothes, or buy them a personal present. Her emotions are not on the surface and this makes her successful with clients. She is practical and caring in her effective matching of product with client.

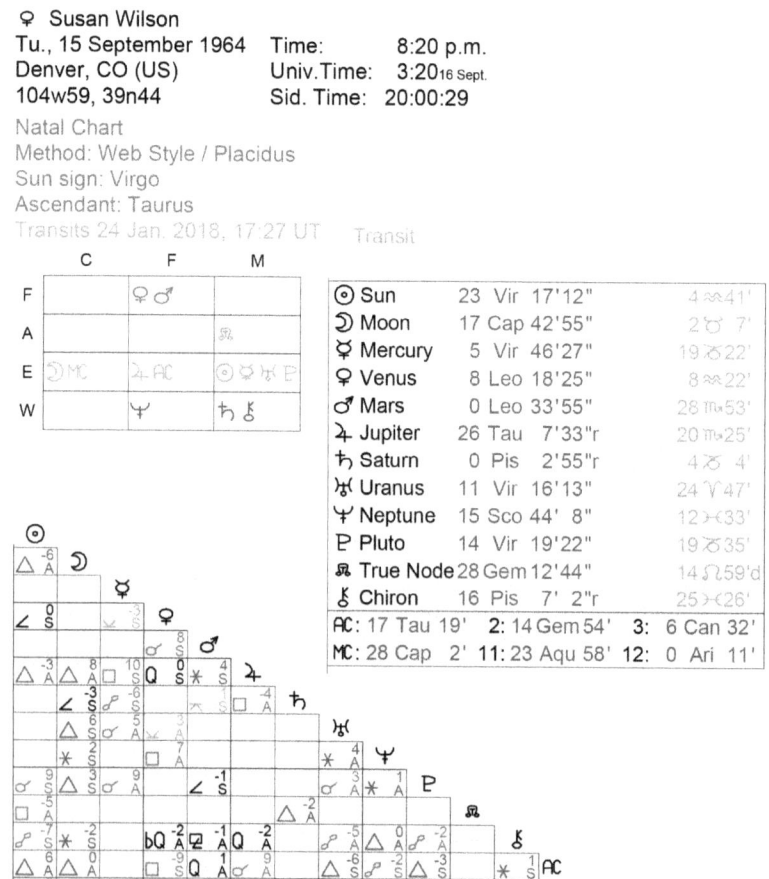

Finally, by having Taurus as her ascendant, or rising sign, she would be steadfast in following through for her work. She would always be there for her work or clients. Yet, no one could push her to go faster. Taurus's are symbolized by the bull because they cannot be deterred from their goals and they cannot be rushed. They also see the beauty in all things. Susan always sees wonderful color and beauty in her surroundings and nature. And she appreciates quality in all material things as well.

That leads us to indicators of past lives in her chart. Her natal chart contains the North Node of the Moon in her second

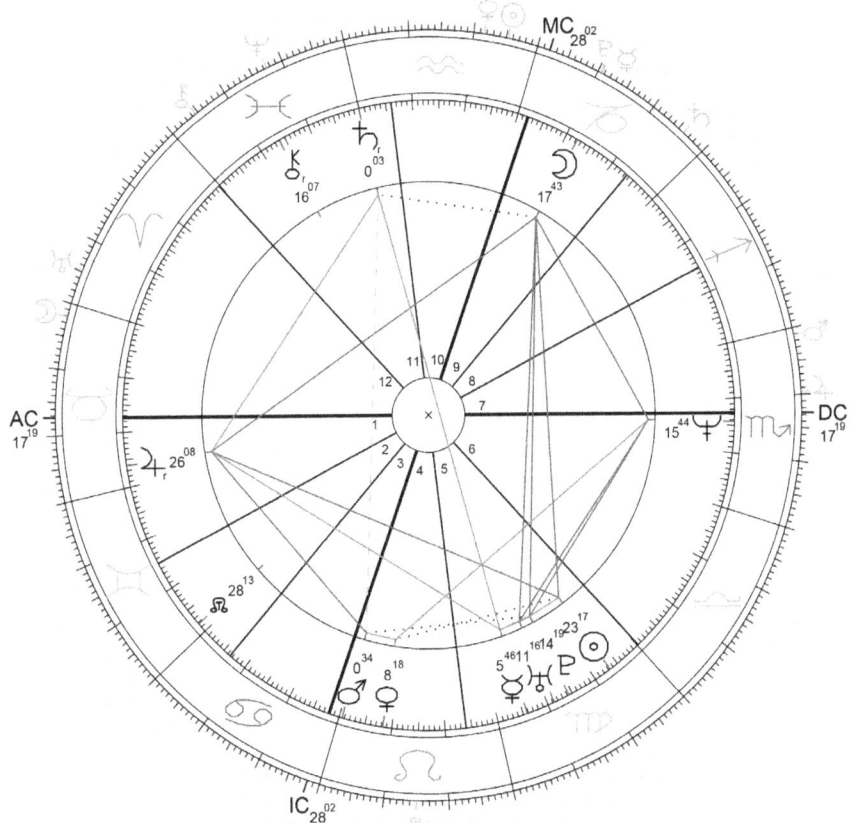

house of money and possessions. That would make her direct opposite house, the eight house, contain her South Node of the Moon. She has come from a most recent life where her decisions were made for her. Her monetary means were provided for her. She was not allowed or exposed to the experience of making her own financial decisions. I call this being invisible to the group that she was surrounded by. Whether she was a ranch hand, a housemaid, or even in a religious sect, she wasn't dealing with the money and the decisions one makes around money. In her present life, by coming into the second house with her North Node, all that was to change. Her higher-self wanted to learn how to control her destiny concerning money once more. She wanted to be independent and earn her own money, by being ruled by Gemini in the second house. Gemini's are very independent and many times are loners. Yet, they are also friendly, and outgoing. Plus, she would be generous with her earnings to those she cared about. That is another Gemini trait. I know this to be true. Susan is very generous to her three grown sons.

Next we look at the placement of Saturn for an indicator of her most recent past life experience. It is in the eleventh house and is opposing her Mercury. Eleventh house rules values and goals, and also groups, friends and organizations. In her most recent past life, Susan did not have success with groups. Her speaking in front of groups may have landed her in trouble. She may have had no friend she could trust. In this life, she will only have a few close friends because her eleventh house is ruled by Aquarius. Aquarians always look toward the goals of group. They tend to have many acquaintances but few really close friends.

Her Saturn in the eleventh house makes her leery of trusting most people. Fears that occurred in the past life dealing with other people may have landed her in a weak place. Also, by having Saturn opposing Mercury, her communication planet, in her fifth house of creativity, she plans on changing that in this present life. Oppositions are an aspect that causes a tension between the two planets as they are 180 degrees from each other. They "tug" at each other to accomplish the task of overcoming a weakness that the soul wants to master. Saturn opposing Mercury would tell us that the lesson of Saturn is to "pull" at her communication ability, Mercury, to speak up more in her current life.

Susan told me that as a young child she told her family she wanted to be a speaker in front of a large audience. She never really understood why she had such a desire to speak to groups before. Now we know that the Saturn opposing Mercury aspect is at work in her life today to make her a strong presence in front of groups to achieve her soul's path.

In this life, Susan has spoken to CEOs, CFOs and leaders of major companies many times in her work. She speaks with confidence from the experience of her years in the software industry. These indicators tell us that the soul of Susan means to turn her past life experience around. She intends to replace the invisible role she played into an important one in this life. How she communicates to others and what she says to others will be well thought out and very deliberate with the help of the groundedness of Saturn when she speaks to groups. From the session with her guides, we now know she will be spreading light to others as well.

Capricorn, ruler of Saturn, rules her ninth house of travel, higher education, and higher consciousness and is another indicator of Susan's most recent past life. Her spiritual modes of communication, tarot cards, hands-on healing and premonitional dreams are always going to be from a practical approach. There will be nothing airy-fairy about her delivery of information to others. She enjoys traveling, yet, up to this point, has only allowed herself to travel for work. This would be another very practical way to approach the ninth house. It would feel too frivolous to just travel for fun for Susan. Many times she has spoken to me about her lack of a college education. She has always desired to have that in her resume. In her industry, a college degree was an important asset that she regretted not obtaining. These are all practical Capricorn approaches to the ninth house.

Now, as we look at her chart, we see her Moon also in the ninth house of higher education, higher consciousness, and foreign travel. Susan has an emotional attachment to these themes as well. It's important to know where a person's Moon is in a chart. Our Moon is where we have dreams or hopes of achieving desires we have. For Susan, it would be a hope to travel for fun, have that higher education degree, and connect deeper to her spirituality.

Chiron, the asteroid, known as the wounded healer, finds itself in the eleventh house for Susan, as well as her Saturn. Chiron is the final indicator of what the soul has been working on for several past lives to overcome and process. This location of Chiron would find Susan with a wounded sense of group identity. This could be experienced as a need to conform to the accepted standards of society and/or a hesitation in expressing her own uniqueness while in the presence of others.

I noticed many times when I asked her to repeat her opinion of some subject, she would act defensive. She told me in the session that something within her felt threatened. It may be that she was punished in her past life or lives for her opinions or actions.

As I mention earlier, Chiron's influence in a chart can be from wounds over many lifetimes. Susan may have been focusing on gaining her strength in front of groups for several lives, not just her most recent one. To be heard and listened to in her present life is very strong in her personality.

Another indicator of her soul's path is the aspect of Neptune squaring her Venus, while also sextiling her Moon and Uranus. A sextile is a sixty degree apart aspect between two planets. The two planets always work harmoniously with each other in this aspect. Success can be found for the person using the energies of the two planets. A square is a ninety degree apart aspect between two planets that force the person to face issues and in the process grow from it.

The square of Neptune and Venus can be found in the charts of spiritual students. It is an important incarnation because the person has to learn to turn the desire for personal love into a universal sense of love and compassion. The soul does not attract personal love until these goals are met. Susan has suffered in personal love earlier in her life and has not had a partner for several years. This square demands that she transform from within before she can sustain a personal love relation.

Susan is very comfortable in her day to day work, which is expressed by her sixth house. Having Neptune in her sixth, she inspires others, she thinks of original ideas, and she emotionally gets involved in coworkers problems. These are all traits that

Neptune, our psychic, intuitive nature, would lend itself to in the day to day workplace. By having Neptune sextile her Moon, Susan would come across to her co-workers and her clients as a sincere and caring person. By also having Neptune sextiling her Uranus as well, Susan has that ability to be original in her ideas. She can think up unusual solutions to the workplace problems for herself and her clients!

Susan wanted to make an impact in this life on others around her. She wanted to be noticed, no matter how uncomfortable it was for her. As I have said before, we choose, as a soul when we are to be born. That creates our planet locations in the chart. Susan has Jupiter in her first house. This gives her an optimistic approach in her attitude at work and around her co-workers. Our first house describes, "Who I am" to others. To others, Susan appears to be confident, optimistic, and open.

We now know that the path is getting clear about Susan's future, so let's take a look at her psychic Tarot card reading. Susan had left her current industry and was hoping for feedback from the reading that this new path would be the brave one to take. I kept seeing that she was approaching her life with a new attitude, (three of Pentacles). The three of Pentacles means she would be using skills that she may not have used for a long time, if at all. In the Judgment card and the Temperance card, I saw that her opportunities would start out slow but would progress by the fall. The Temperance card means to have patience and you will make steady progress. The Judgement card expresses the energy that she will get her due reward after many years of hard work. I did see the Star card for her several times, which tells me that even if a new position isn't the most ideal, Susan will finally be able to relax and enjoy her life more. This is a dream she has had for herself for a long time as one of her goals. The Star card means what we have envisioned as our dreams or goals for the future is coming into view.

In the spring, a few months later, she did find a job in her new location of Colorado Springs working for a local software manufacturer in the restaurant industry. What she did not know is how this less stressful life would be changing her. She later admitted that she was much happier with her life. It was calmer, she was in a quiet neighborhood, and she had some flexibility with her schedule. These things sound small, but to a Virgo, who puts so much pressure on herself to be the best, it was a "big change." What a reward to relax and enjoy her home and the simple things once again. The cards said that she would be ending those 12 hour works days forever, (ten of Swords).

We also asked about "Bear". This would be the man who would enter her life in a year or two that her guides had told her about. The cards agreed that within two years, she would be living a different life as she radiated the light from within to others. The cards didn't specifically express the "Bear" relationship. Through my guides and the reading of the Tarot cards, we saw that Susan's life would be happier, and more fulfilled than she could image right now. The cards of Queen of Pentacles and nine of Cups indicated a great transformation in the months to come. The Queen of Pentacles expresses the energy of Susan, grounded, abundant and connected to the earth. The nine of Cups tells us that what she most wishes for in her life is soon to be felt.

I talked to Susan after our session and she told me of the conversation she was having with her fellow workers that day. She listened to their responsibilities and their challenges. She was informally inspiring them with ideas. One man came up later to tell her how much she had helped him with his challenges and the way he looked at them. He told her he felt much better after their talk. The shift had started!

Chapter Three

Betty Wessling

*The Sales Coach
Learning to Receive*

I met Betty Wessling about seven years ago. Since my earliest past life regression session with her, about three years ago, I'd seen many changes in her perceptions and actions. She has always been a hard worker. She rarely took time off just to "play". If she did play, it was strategic play with perspective clients or peers. Advancing her career was foremost on her mind. Betty is a sales coach by profession and has written four books on the subject. What's unusual about Betty as a sales coach is that she is also intuitive, spiritual and wise. She teaches her clients to work from their hearts as well as their intellects.

This year there was a shift. She started taking most Fridays off from work to "live." Betty started country western dancing a few times a month in the big dance hall in Denver. She told me she was ready for a long term relationship now that she was in her 50s and finding balance in her life. These were signs that something deep within her was changing, letting go, and taking new risks.

Years ago, the past life regression session with Betty provided the foundation for understanding the changes I currently saw in her. In that regression, Betty saw herself in a traumatic past life in the early 1800s where she was married with two children. The farm house and surrounding property were not attended to by her husband. The burden of family and home weighed on the shoulders of this woman that Betty recognized as her soul essence.

One day the house caught on fire, the family almost perished as immediate fire aid was not available in that countryside where they lived. The husband was sent to prison for his negligence and she was separated from her children. For the rest of her life, in that time period, Betty's soul felt so guilty that she rarely connected to her children. She lived out her days alone on a small farm with a few animals. At the end of her life her spirit guides told her that she failed to achieve much in that life because she had been so traumatized from the house fire. She simply "dropped out". This information is useful for a greater understanding of the session today.

As Betty begun the induction with me, she saw bright lights and was told her guides were meeting her to begin this past life. That is always a good sign. Betty's guides want to make sure she is not frightened or afraid to make this journey, so they make her feel their presence around her at the start. She saw an old room that was very cold. It had old furniture and antiques, she said. Betty saw herself in a living room alone. When asked what she was wearing, Betty described she was wearing pants and a blouse. Next, she said she felt like there was someone behind her, but she couldn't describe them. Her hair was put up and she said she was 70 years old. Her name was Diane and she was in Tennessee in 1866.

Betty said that Diane was just walking around the house looking at pictures on the wall. She sees one of her grandmother. She said that the house belonged to her, Diane's, grandmother. She knows that Diane loves her grandmother and is very close to her. She said her parents also live there, but they are gone at the time. She seemed to have a distant relationship with her parents.

We move to the next most significant scene, and Betty sees that Diane is cooking for the family. She is married now with three kids. When asked if she recognized the souls of the children as anyone she knew today, Betty said they were her niece and nephews, Jack, Michael, and Layla.

She saw the kids having fun just coloring in books. She said her husband was gone and she was happy about that. (What we have done is start the regression at a mature age, and then backtracked to the same life, but at a much younger age. Many times the scenes go in this sequence. I believe that is to calm the person down before an intense scene is shown.)

Next scene is of Diane hanging laundry on the same day. Betty sees that she begins to scream. One of the kids has fallen into the water. One of the boys, the five year old, is drowning. Diane tries to get him out. Her husband comes home, and he is running over to her and the boy. But the boy is limp by the time he gets to him. Now Betty sees that the husband is fighting with Diane because he blames her for the death of their son. Betty sees that the husband is the soul essence of James. James was a man she had a long term relationship with when she was younger in her present life.

Diane feels her husband is terribly mean to her. He blames her for the death. The whole relationship between them changes. The next scene Betty sees is of Diane in the same house in the kitchen. She is in her 40s. The kids are ten and twelve now and at the table. But all of them are sadder now. The husband is outside. He has no peace in his mind, and he is drinking a lot. Betty says the energy in the room is heavy. Diane feels there is nothing to live for.

Next, Diane is on a train and she is in her early 50s. She left her husband, and split from their marriage. She is finally smiling. She has on a blue dress and hat. She is going to a town to take care of people in a home. Diane finally has her life back. She does feel distant from her children, but they are on their own and she knows they are fine. Diane is finally safe from her husband.

Now, Betty sees herself as Diane once again in her 70s as we saw in the first scene starting the regression. There is dancing going on around her. She is dancing with a man. He is a new man to the area and his name is Jack. Betty does not recognize the soul essence of this man in her present life. Diane is smiling with joy and she is laughing. (Remember how Betty likes to country western two-step in her present life and the joy it brings her.) Betty sees that the two end up together. She also sees that her Mother lives in a room in the home where Diane works tending to the elderly.

I ask Betty to go to Diane's very last day, and she sees her in a bed. She is 102 years old. It would have been around the year 1900 when Diane was passing at age of 102. Betty felt that Diane was certainly rewarded in the last part of her life. She sees that Diane laughed a lot and had people around her that she cared for.

At the end of the life, I asked her to bring through her son Jack and ask him about his early death at age five. She asked why he left so soon. He told her he had to go. He had to get her away from her husband and his father.

She also asked the older man Jack, who she dated in later years and had so much fun with to come through and talk to her. He said it was a pleasure to be with her, and that he loved her. He went on to say that he would meet her in her current life soon.

When I asked Betty to discover her soul's purpose in that life, she said that it was to discover joy. She said that she accomplished that when she moved and left her husband. Those later years were most joyful.

The second past life Betty experienced that day was an overlapping parallel life. The scene began with a woman walking down the street, and she stopped as she talked to four men in a car. They were construction workers, and seem to be flirting with her. She was flirting back. This lady was in her 30s, dressed in boots and a dress. Her hair was up in a bun on top of her head with long curly parts of her hair hanging down on the sides. Betty told me the lady she saw as herself was named Lisa, and she was in Colorado. The year was 1952.

The next scene has Lisa at a counter, she is working in a diner as a waitress. She goes over to a table full of men and begins to flirt with them as she takes their orders. She writes her phone number on the back of the receipt as she gives it to one of the men at the table. Betty feels that excitement that Lisa feels at the time. Lisa thinks she has a fun life talking and flirting with the men. Now Betty sees that Lisa has started to date the man from the diner. His name is Marcus. She does not recognize his soul essence as anyone she knows in her current life. They go to movies, lunch, and dancing. They are not married, but they are together as a couple. Lisa is very happy.

Then Lisa receives a phone call. Marcus was hit by a car while he was walking in the street, and he has been killed. Lisa is crushed and brokenhearted! They had only been together for nine months when the accident happened. Lisa is just devastated and retreats from everything. She quits her job. She is so sad. She is lonely, and only goes out to two or three places for errands and comes back home each week. She is living on her savings as she grieves. Betty says that she sees that Lisa was reclusive for almost a year to get over her grief. Finally, she is forced to go back to work.

Lisa is now selling clothes in a dress shop. She is 45 years old. She is starting to smile again. She is starting to see her girlfriends again. She attends a party. Betty can see her mingling, drinking, and having fun. She meets Kevin there. She likes him, and they start dating. He has lost his wife, and he has three little kids. It is hard with the children. They miss mom terribly. Lisa and Kevin never become romantically close. They are just friends and companions for each other.

Betty now sees that she is in her 60s. She quit dating Kevin, but they are still friends. Betty says she is not spiritual at all and the only interest she takes up in later life is singing. She joins a choir. On her last day, Lisa is sitting and drinking tea. She goes to the couch and falls asleep. She simply never wakes up. She was seventy-two years old.

I calculated that the year Lisa passed was 1992. When I ask Betty what has happening in her life in 1992, she told me she was going through a lot of change. I find that overlapping parallel lives divide the soul's energy on Earth. When one passes, all the energy of that life now goes into the remaining soul's energy in the still living human. Many times the goals of one life cause the energy to shift greatly for the remaining life's path.

Betty said that in 1992 she was about to move to Colorado from New Jersey where she has grown up. She had a skiing accident while she was still in New Jersey. That accident slowed her down for three years in her plans to move. Those three years really got Betty on a different track, she said. Betty said that period when she had to lay low opened her eyes to manifesting what she truly wanted in her life. In 1995 Betty moved to Colorado with a renewed jest for life. She had goals to be a woman that would make a difference in other's lives. This is something that Lisa never considered. It seems that Lisa's experiences have caused the soul to radically change Betty. Betty now has the drive to achieve much more than originally planned. The part of her soul that had been in Lisa's life was there now to help Betty rise to a higher level of consciousness than Lisa had ever achieved.

When I asked Betty what had been the soul's purpose of Lisa's life, she said it was to find love. She said Lisa had that for nine months of her life. So Lisa felt she had achieved her goal in that life. She wasn't necessarily spiritual, but to feel the love that she and Marcus had for nine months was her greatest joy.

Next we had the meeting with Betty's spirit guides. "Jane" was a kind, loving, and witty spirit guide in her 50s. She was dressed in a pink gown with long hair. Jane said she had been Betty's Master Guide in the two past lives Betty just saw.

Another guide came through named Carly. She was a strong, capable guide in her 30s that was very business-like.

As Betty asked her guides why she was shown these two particular lives, she was told by her guides that they were very complicated lives. Betty's soul had chosen hard, sad, and often lonely experiences. Betty asked, "Can we have a loving relationship in my present life now?" Her guides told her yes. She had asked for those lives to learn about the human condition when it must suffer and be alone. These hard lessons gave Betty the ability to coach people today in her present life because she understands what they are feeling and the pain they have endured in their lives. This is the reason all of us, as souls, come back again and again in incarnations. We are learning the lessons of a being a soul on Earth in order to help others advance in their learning through being a teacher, an instructor, or a mentor in whatever we do.

In 2017, Betty's guides told her that she would meet the soul essence of Marcus from Lisa's life. He was coming back to be with her in her present life. She would be meeting him in the fall of 2017. Lisa told me that she was going on a spiritually based cruise with a large group that followed the teachings of Esther Hicks. Esther Hicks channels Abraham, an advanced being. Betty said that Esther Hicks would be leading seminars during the entire cruise. Jane told her that on this trip she would meet the man who is the soul essence of Marcus. He is on the cruise as well. He would be as involved in spiritual growth as she was.

Lisa was asked by her guides if she was going to give Marcus a chance. She had allowed very few men into her life so far. Betty felt she was ready and really had been working on herself to be open and ready for a long-term relationship. Her guides told her it would be challenging at first. The man lived in a different state. They told her she would be willing to move to be with him. They told her she would marry this man.

When Lisa asked why it had taken so long for her to be ready, she was told that the past life we had seen several years ago where she had almost lost her two children to a fire by her husband's negligence had really caused her to need quite a bit of healing. Betty had been working on that healing in this life especially. She adored children, and even volunteered at the Down's Syndrome Association. Her nephew has Down's Syndrome. She also recognized him as one of her children in the past life regression concerning the fire. She was now ready to be open to love again.

We were now ready to look at Betty's Astrology Natal Chart to see if the soul's plan to come into this life backed up everything we just saw in her two past live regression experiences.

Betty has a Sun in Capricorn, a moon in Aquarius, and a rising sign in Libra. This "skeleton" told us much about who Betty is at her core. She is hard working and will always follow through on her projects. There is not a harder working Sun sign than Capricorn. By having a rising sign of Libra, she chose to be a fair and balanced person to the outside world. Libra risings usually are very attractive people. Betty is a very healthy, fit, and attractive woman. She looks much younger than her age. Libras are very aggressive in getting things done. They are a cardinal sign, as is Capricorn. I have seen that when Betty takes on a project, nothing can stop her. She would be a good person to have on any committee. She would do her part and never let anyone down in accomplishing her responsibilities.

In the chart attached, one can see many challenges that Betty brought into her life in her present incarnation. She wanted, as a soul, to be pushed beyond what Lisa or Diane had attempted to do in their lives. First of all, by having Neptune in her first house makes her extremely intuitive and psychic. As I got to know Betty, I could see this trait used in all she did for her clients. She could read their needs so well. Next, Neptune squares* her Moon and Saturn. This would cause her to not

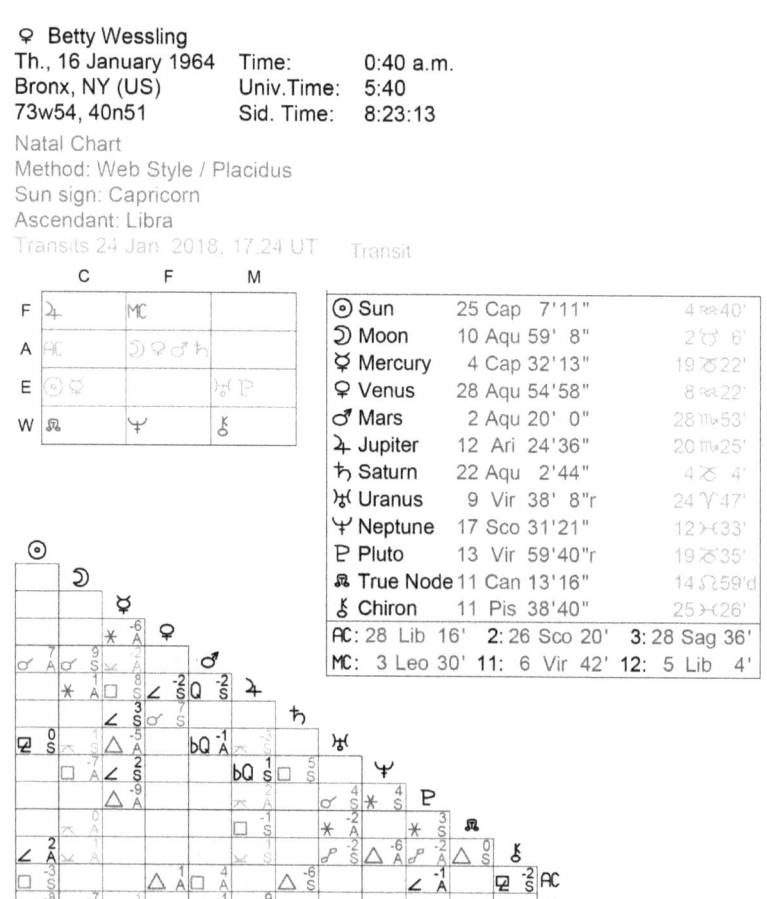

see her relationships clearly with the male partners in her life. Even her relationship with her father would be hindered by this aspect. In her younger years she may have been disappointed and let down by the men in her life when she discovered they were not all she had supposed they were. Neptune makes our emotions sometimes "fuzzy" and unclear about others. The square to her Moon means she came to clear up the fear of close

Square: When two planets are 90 degrees apart. Squares are dynamic. They force you to face issues and in the process you grow.

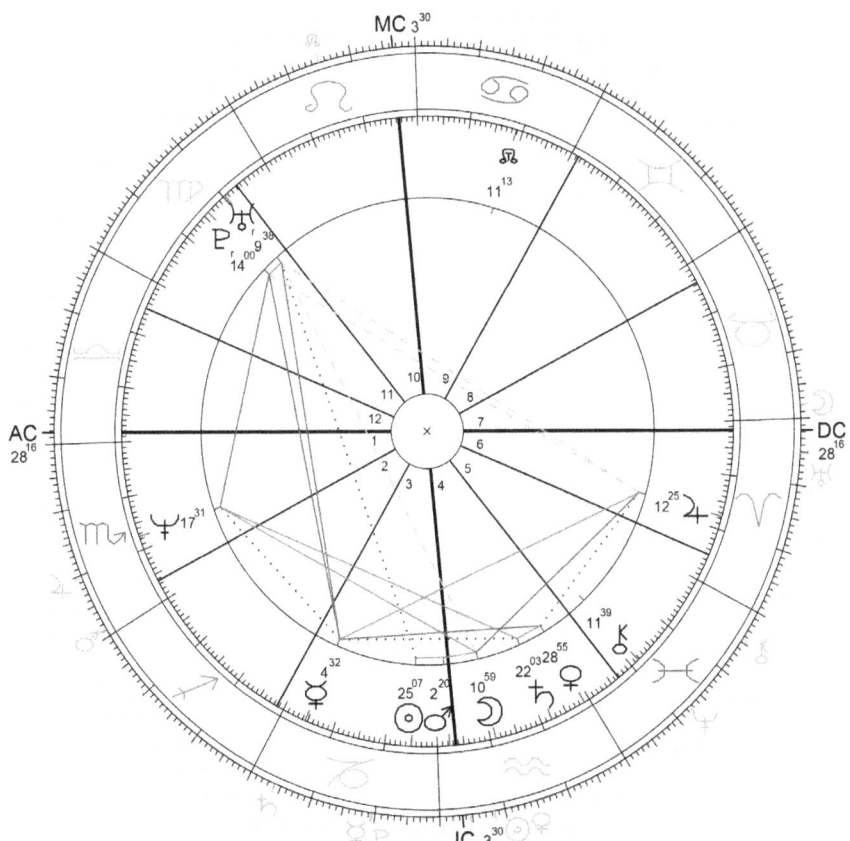

relationships in this life. The square to her Saturn will keep her grounded and persevering as she makes her way through the fear and uncertainty of her emotions in a close relationship.

In her second house, there is a strong trine between her Mercury in the third house of communication and her Pluto and Uranus in the eleventh house of groups and committees, and goals. Betty would be excellent in speaking before groups to empower her audience. She would be a good leader. She would also be a good writer, good social media creator, and teacher. All of these features she has in her life, and she makes her living from them. As I mentioned earlier, she has completed four books on her coaching subject. Mercury is our planet of communication and it is placed in the house of communication. Betty's soul was determined she would be a voice that was heard in this present life. Pluto and Uranus would make it unique and dynamic!

Concerning past lives we must look at the location of Saturn. Saturn is in Betty's fourth house of home. This usually means that an opposite sex parent has given her many hard challenges in a past life or lives. In this life as she was coming into birth, she looked to see her parents and her soul said, "Oh no, not him again as my father." And in her present life, her father really pushed her hard as she was growing up. He seemed to have a drive to push her more than her other three sisters. Could it have been this previous past life together that reminded him of how hard he had been on her, and he decided to repeat it? The ruler of Saturn is Capricorn, and Capricorn rules no houses in her chart. It is a "hidden" sign in her houses. Meaning, she came in with much reservation about repeating these learning lessons with the soul essence of her father today.

Chapter 3 - Betty Wessling

We look at the placement of Chiron as well for past life information in the chart. In her fifth house of creativity, children, and projects, Chiron is ruled by Pisces. Pisces is the most psychic and emotional signs of the zodiac. Chiron asked Betty to go through these many hard challenges in her present life, and also the past lives of Diane and Lisa to learn the hard way what human life is all about. However, in Betty's life, Pisces asked her to raise her consciousness to understand that we are all here to help each other and become one. The best way to do that is to put your soul to the test by enduring many different experiences. We saw just two. This soul is ready to teach people a higher meaning of living on this planet.

Finally we see that with Betty's Sun, Mercury, and Mars all in the third house of communication, Betty was destined to shine in her life. With the energy of Mars, the planet that helps us get what we want out of life, conjuncting* her Sun, Betty will shine whenever she communicates and teaches others of life. Betty, with these three most important planets in her house of communication, is most comfortable, being a teacher and a motivator.

The North and South Nodes for Betty are in her Ninth and Third house. As I have mentioned before in this book, where the Moon's nodes are located in a natal chart explains the most recent past life and why a soul came into this incarnation by the houses they are located in. By having her South node in her third house, Betty came from a most recent past life, being

Conjunction: When planets in a chart are within 10 degrees of each other. This aspect emphasizes the qualities of the two planets. They become more prominent and powerful. It may be harmonious or inharmonious, according to the planets involved.

Lisa or Diane, where her voice wasn't heard. She just followed along in society to get through life. She was not a person who made a difference in anyone's life, except maybe her children's. In her present life, with the North Node in her ninth house of higher consciousness, travel, higher education, and publishing, she has found her home. In this life she is heard and read. She does travel to her clients for trainings and teachings. She is published and listened to in all that she does. Plus, she is delving into spirituality as never before. Lisa and Diane never chose to raise their consciousness or speak up and be heard. They simply led simple lives and looked for love and enjoyment like singing and dancing to answer all their joy and happiness needs.

Betty is breaking out of that mold and is using all her strengths in this life. With the Sun and Mars in her third house of communication, her intuitive strengths being enhanced with Neptune being placed in her first house and Chiron placed in her fifth house which is ruled by Pisces, Betty is deemed to be skillful at professional coaching. The only thing she is missing is the long term relationship. Betty's soul wanted to make sure she was balanced in this present life before she concentrated on a long term relationship.

Let's see what the psychic reading can tell us about her future. I asked Betty's guides through the tarot cards to tell us how her next six months looked. We were asking to see into the future from February through August. I use the Celtic Cross spread to interpret the question plus I pulled four extra cards for what the client is thinking and four extra cards above the final 10th card to help flush out the final card's meaning.

I knew Betty was venturing into a specialized type of coaching. She was starting a coaching practice that catered to attorneys only. She said they are so in their heads about their work, they fail to feel the empathy for their clients that they need to gain new accounts. She was to be the teacher to change that thought process. Not many in her field were attempting such a hard market as attorneys. But Betty was not to be deterred as she connected on Linkedin and other business connectors like attorney's journals and periodicals in her advertising.

While she was changing her career, she was also beginning the freer thoughts of just having fun in her life. Instead of going to dating websites, where she had been in the past, she felt she was going to meet her long term partner doing what she enjoyed doing, dancing, being with friends and traveling.

The cards said just the same. I was getting the ten of Swords. I call this card the "slamming of the door and locking it with a key" card. No longer will a person do what they were doing or working in the same manner. They have moved forward and will not return to this type of living again. I saw that in both her business life and her personal life. She was eager to step into the new field of helping attorneys. Though Betty would still keep her present clients and work with them, she wanted to walk this new path. The same can be said for Betty's ways to meet a partner. She agreed. I saw the Crumbing Tower card. It reveals that everything in her present life is going to be changing. Not to return to the old. This would reply to the old way of meeting dates through the dating websites. She had not been ready to meet someone in the past when she was using the websites. But now she had reached a level in her career where she was allowing herself to play and enjoy life more. Now would be her best time to meet someone.

I also saw the ten of Wands, meaning she was still placing her career as her number one priority, even though Betty denied that when I asked her if that was true. I also was seeing the six of Pentacles which implies that it is okay to work hard, but you must remember your loved ones and friends and give them equal importance.

I also saw the three of Swords. This would tell me that Betty is very happy being on her own in her work, but not so in her private life. She is now ready to find a partner, but I see that the Star card is also present. She wants her partner to have similar goals as she has. She wants all her hard work to reward her in her future and he, hopefully, feels the same way about his hard work in whatever profession he has.

I still kept seeing that over the summer her business was going to bring her much success. I kept getting the death card and the Ace of Pentacles. Both of these cards tell me that she is going to radically be changing her approach to clients and the type of work that she does, but she is going to be seeing much financial success for her efforts.

Now, I move to September and when she would be on her cruise. All the cards are different. I received the king of Swords for Betty. This would be a man that is a hard worker, makes decisions, and is a little cool in his show of affection. He might even had a previous career in law enforcement or been in the military. I saw that Betty feels disappointed as she begins the cruise because she has not met anyone over the summer by pulling the five of Cups card.

But, ever hopeful, Betty keeps being given the ten of Cups. She wants the whole package. A committed relationship like a marriage, or a full time relationship that would feel like a marriage. She wants to know she can trust and be supported by this man, her partner.

I move to the fall after the cruise and all the cards change. She has met him. I get the moon, the eight of Cups and two of Cups. She is thinking about him, (Moon Card), and she is ready to put part of her life behind her to go forward with this opportunity, (eight of Cups), and she feels they really connected like close friends.

And finally, I see the Death card again, the Devil card, and King of Wands. This would mean that they are connecting after the cruise and he is changing her life. I let the Devil card mean passion for me, so that would tell me that she has great passion and love for this man. The King of Wands would tell me he is an entrepreneur, thinks outside the box, and is a multi-tasker. This man is much like Betty is in her life!

Going forward, it looks like the cards just confirmed all that Betty's spirit guides told her at the end of her session. She will be meeting "Marcus". When you meet a "soul contract", a person immediately knows that this connection "feels" different. It is supposed to feel familiar so that a soul will not casually walk away from the opportunity. This connection is planned for the soul's growth of both people.

Chapter Four

Martha Shaffer

The Crusader and Teacher

Martha Shaffer was one of the first people I met when I moved from Sarasota, Florida, in 1999, to the tiny, mountain town of Crestone, Colorado. The town is maybe 1500 population when there is a Buddhist retreat going on in the mountains. Most of the time it is just several hundred people made up of Buddhists, Japanese Shumee followers, and Christians. There is also a part of the population that has just "dropped out" and wants to be under the radar. I left my Sales Manager job in Building in Florida to expressly develop my spiritual abilities in Crestone. Martha and her former husband, Doug, were drawn to Crestone for spiritual reasons as well. Both practice Buddhism which was a popular practice in Crestone.

    I tell you all this to explain why you find these highly educated residents in Crestone. Martha came to this small rural mountain town with a Master's degree in Contemplative Psychotherapy and additional training in non-profit board governance, massage therapy and holistic health. The winters are cold and isolating. From Crestone, it is fifty miles to the nearest town of Salida, Colorado. Many people were like me and looking for a raising of their consciousness by being in such a high vibrational community. That is what drew myself, Martha, Doug, and many of the friends I met there. But after eight and a half years in Crestone as a general contractor of Lee Mitchell Homes, I felt I had achieved all I came to do. I moved to Salida first, and later to Denver to start my spiritual career in past life regression.

Martha moved away, relocated to Boulder, even moved to Arkansas for a short time, and has now returned to Crestone. Something always keeps drawing her back. That is one of her questions for me in the session.

Martha agreed to do a past life regression because she had questions about what her path was in her present role as a trainer and coach to the local school board and Charter School of "Policy Governance," a governance model that promotes sound leadership practices. Soon after her return to Crestone, she had become active in the Crestone End of Life Project, CEOLP. CEOLP provides education in death and dying, and offer services for end of life. Martha wondered if the path of service and trainer in these roles in Crestone was truly what she had returned in this life to achieve.

Another one of her questions in the intake part of the session was to understand why she felt so much fear about Trump and his presidency. Martha said it reminded her of the World War II past life we had seen a few years back where she had been working against Nazism as a woman from Poland.

She also had a question about her future. Where would she be going next after Crestone? She did not feel that Crestone, Colorado would be her forever home. And finally, would she have a life-long partner. She had long ago divorced her husband, Doug, but had remained close friends as both still lived in Crestone.

As she began the scene in the regression, she saw a wooded area next to a railroad track. She was in a field close to the woods. Next she heard a noise. The sound was man-made. It sounded like machinery, Martha said. She could smell unpleasant smells. Burn smells, not good, she said. The burn smells bring up fear in her immediately.

I asked her to describe her clothing. She described her boots as being felt with leather on the soles of the boots. The boots were well used, she said. She was wearing leggings with a skirt over them. She was also wearing a coat that had a hood on it, and her hair was put up under the hood. She went on to describe herself as a woman of thirty-five with red hair. Martha said her name was Hannah. When I asked her what country she saw Hannah in, Martha clearly said Austria. When I asked her the year, she replied that it was 1939.

Martha said that Hannah is listening for a train that is coming. She felt Hannah was catching up with people she was supposed to meet. She didn't want to miss this train. These people are the next place for her to find safety.

Now, Hannah sees that it is getting dark. Either she missed the train or she will still meet them. The train signifies death, but Hannah doesn't know that yet, Martha said. Hannah doesn't know what the people she is to meet look like. Next, she hears voices. She crouches down. She doesn't know if she wants them to see her. Next, she hears the train. Hannah can tell the voices are coming from the woods. She doesn't feel safe with the voices. Next, she hears the train getting louder. She gets really small as she crouches more.

The train arrives. It rumbles as it arrives. It's now beyond dusk but still not totally dark. Hannah hears sounds from the train. It is not a passenger train. It finally travels on. After the train is gone, Hannah no longer hears any voices in the area. She decides to stand up. It's now very dark. Martha says that Hannah does not know what to do now. She is hungry, she thinks. She feels it's going to be cold tonight as well. She sees a small light coming along the track by the field side. She feels it is ok. Hannah walks toward it. The light is coming from a lantern of sorts. It is held up, not down. She trusts it. She is crouched down. Hannah doesn't want to cause alarm, if it's a friend. She makes a hissing sound. They stop. There is more than one of them. There are three of them. One of them is a young man dressed in country attire. One of them is a woman. The third man has a rifle.

Hannah knows the name of one of them. She knows the woman. She gets up and goes with them. They feed her. Hannah is now running from Hitler's soldiers. Martha says that Hannah is from Poland. It is her home country. She is Jewish. They are Jewish and married to Jewish. Hannah sleeps there for the night. It's a two room farmhouse with a light on, but no fire. It is cold. Hannah will be leaving tomorrow.

I ask Martha to take us to the next most significant scene for Hannah in this past life during World War II. (This is the same life we visited a few years ago, but saw very little of Hannah's life. Today, Martha was ready to see much more about this very traumatic life during the war as part of the Resistance.) Now, Hannah, in the next scene, is a few years older. She looks worn, Martha says. She is in a city now. The city is devastated from the bombings of the war. Hannah is part of a Resistance group in the city. They help move people. They blow up bridges against Hitler's soldiers. They are even known to ambush the soldiers on the roads. They can even tap into the radio signals of the German army.

Martha says that these people in the Resistance are like her family now. She, as Hannah, feels very tired. She smokes a lot. People come to her for help. Hannah is tired and doesn't go out much from her safe place in the underground.

Hannah's breathing has been compromised by the coal smoke she is forced to inhale so often. The coal dust pollutes the air. She feels herself coughing a great deal.

Martha saw that she was shot in the leg as Hannah. She received a bullet to her right leg. I asked her if her leg gives her trouble in her present life, and Martha said that it gets numb and is very painful. I know that Martha for most of her life has suffered greatly with her lungs. Each winter in Crestone, she usually has a bad cough and a cold of some kind. Martha always wears a scarf around her neck. When I am told of a physical ailment in the past life, I always stop and ask the client if they suffer any pain in that same area, and most often the answer is yes. The results of this most dangerous past life that Martha experienced as Hannah, have today weakened her DNA as she reincarnated as Martha.

In the city, Hannah's job is to strategize from this hub. She is in the major city of London. Now the year is 1944, Martha says. She sees that Hannah cares for someone deeply. It is a woman named Rosa. Today, Martha identifies the soul energy of Rosa as her dear friend Tamar, who also lives in Crestone.

In the next scene, Martha sees that Hannah is lying in bed with blankets over her. She has fever and she is coughing. She is very ill. She is having trouble breathing. She is not alone, but with friends around her. She is so tired. Hannah accepts her dying, Martha notes. The year is 1945.

She sees two people there who give her tea and hold her head up. They keep her warm. As she leaves her body she says goodbye to her friends, and they say they love her and call her "Mother."

When I asked Martha to ask her higher-self what was her soul's purpose in coming into that very difficult in WWII, Martha replied that she was there to share a sense of peace and compassion in the face of conflict. She was also there to take action and help the Resistance.

As I checked the years, I see that Martha as Hannah passed in 1945. As the soul of Martha, she was born in 1953. This was her most previous past life. That is why the fear of Trump's commands remind her of Nazism and the fear of the German war. Because the fear is so recent, out of habit, the soul feels the fear again regardless if it is warranted.

As we left that life, Martha commented that she had always felt that she was born into the "wrong time". She said that she was born too late. She liked the quality of life in a past time. She longed for a peaceful community of Jewish and Christian people that supported each other. She now feels that that is what Hannah had in her home in Poland before the war. She was torn away from that small village life and never got to return to that life of peace.

As I inducted Martha into her second past life, she saw rolling hills and open prairie land. She sees herself walking and the sun is strong and high. She is a man, a young man, who is Native American. He has on leather pants below the knee and a shirt with no sleeves. He has his hair tied back in one braid. He has on boots up to his knees. Martha says he is in his late 20s. She sees that he is carrying arrows in a pouch and holding a bow. When I asked his name, she said, "Blue Eyes." His parents didn't have blue eyes, but his grandparents did. His grandfather was a white trapper. It is the 1870-1880s, and the white man is taking over the plains and killing all the buffaloes. When I asked what state Blues Eyes was in, Martha said, "South Dakota."

Martha said Blue Eyes was out patrolling the area. He was looking for a herd of buffaloes, and to see if the white men were in the area. Martha sees that he returns to the village and reports to the tribal leaders. They are camped at the river. He has a sweetheart, but they are not married. Her name is Little Deer. She is very loving to Blue Eyes. She fixes him food, and she gives him shelter when he is in the camp. Martha sees that Little Deer is the soul essence of Doug, her ex-husband. I asked her to contact her higher-self and ask if this was Doug's most recent past life, and she said, "yes."

Because their world was coming to an end, they did not marry. The tribe was always on the move. The next scene Martha sees is of Little Eyes being a spokesperson for his tribe to the American officials. He is trying to save them from being moved off the land. He can see that he is not being listened to by the white officials. He and all the other leaders of the Native Americans can see where this is going. They hold their dignity even though they know they will die.

The next scene has the tribe in Canada. They are being chased. He and his tribe get to Canada, but many die on the way. The winter conditions are very harsh. Little Deer dies along the trail. There is a great displacement going on for all the tribes. There is a great sense of loss everywhere in the Indian Nation. Blue Eyes is now 48 years old. He is at the end of his life. It is the 1890s. He has a sense that he must help set up a safe place for anyone that is left there. He reaches out to meet the local natives. No one from his tribe survives the winter.

It's his last day, Martha says. He is next to a tree. He is freezing to death. He has animal skins covering him, but it is no help. He is sick and exhausted. There is no one to build a fire for him. He chose to be alone to die, she says. He looks up to the heavens and says thank you to Great Spirit who protected his tribe all these years.

He tells the spirit of Little Deer that she reminded him of joy. He tells her it was a good and courageous life for both of them.

When I asked Martha to connect with her higher-self about her soul's purpose in that Native American life, she replied that it was to serve as a bridge in an attempt to be a human being to the white man. She said Blue Eyes helped the best he could.

We invited in Martha's Master Guide to help us. Martha saw her as a strong female energy. She sees clearly, is compassionate, and fierce, with a sharp sense of humor. She appeared to be in her 60s with something in her hair. It went around her head and held a band of feathers on one side of her head. She had shoulder length hair and it was silver gray. She wore a tunic top with long sleeves and gaucho pants with boots underneath the pants. When I asked her what the master guide would like to be called, Martha said, "Mary." A second guide also came through, and Martha saw him as tall and lanky. He was quiet and measured when he spoke. He name was George.

We asked her master guide Mary why she had been shown the two particular past lives that day. She answered through Martha that she was learning courage and patience to follow her inner intuition in both of them. She was developing her intuition even more in her present life. She was also developing her ability to teach and work for the good of the whole in the two past lives and in her present life as well. This is a goal of her soul that has taken many lives to master. She needed to see these two past lives to understand this very important path she chose.

When we asked Mary if Crestone was to be Martha's home, her master guide replied that it has a purpose. She said that there will be other places that will call Martha. She said that Martha will move in and out of Crestone. It is a base camp for her. Some of her best friends have homes there. Mary, her guide, encourages Martha to hold steady. It will become clear very soon where she is headed next. She said that part of the holding steady idea is the practice of being patient and the practice of using her intuition.

We did receive a request from Mary, her guide, to perform an attachment release on the trauma of Hannah's life for Martha.

She was still suffering several physical problems because of it. After performing the light healing treatment for Martha, her master guide said that it will help her immensely in the future. As the pain dissolves, Martha will become more focused and clear, Mary said.

Finally, we asked about any future long term companion for Martha. Her guides told her there is a small group of family and friends that will always play a close role in her life. This circle is her family. None of these people will be hers alone, but the group will bring her much love. Her guides told Martha that she will always be cared for financially, physically and emotionally. "This is who you are as a soul. You do this in many lives."

Martha had many of her answers by viewing these two very important past lives, but I wanted to confirm that the astrology natal chart showed this crusader path in her present life as well.

As you can see in the attached astrological natal chart for Martha Shaffer, She is a Gemini with a Virgo Rising and a Libra Moon, (The basic "Skeleton" I have mentioned before). But what is most interesting about her planets is that her Sun is on the cusp of the house of Gemini and Cancer at 29 degrees Gemini. The Cusp is the dark line separating one house from another. If a planet is with 5 degrees of that line, we call it "on the Cusp". In Martha's case, her sun personality will show traits of both of the signs, Gemini and Cancer.

That means that Martha certainly will have traits of a Gemini, but she may also be much like a Cancer in her actions. I have found that to be true in Martha's nature. Gemini represents the conscious mind. Geminis flit from one situation to another in order to gain growth through may varied experiences. You must appeal to them through logic, for they are not a sign that makes decisions based on emotion. The sign represents wit and a sense of humor. Geminis are adverse to close and binding ties. They also need a vocation in which they can move about and mingle with people. All these describe Martha. However, with the sun on the cusp of Cancer, she may be similar to Cancer in many ways. Cancers are mothering, sustaining and nurturing. Cancer people live much in their feelings and affections. Cancer is a subconscious sign. Everything is latent and hidden. Like the crab who sidesteps any object approaching him, Cancerians are not forthright and direct in action. There is an indefiniteness and an apparently vague subtlety which proves most elusive to people dealing with Cancerians. All I have found to be true in Martha's personality.

Now moving to her Virgo rising. She is a hard worker, extremely honest, and very critical of herself in all her performances. All of these are traits you find in Virgo personalities. Remember that the rising sign is our outside armor. So she "appears' that way to her co-workers and friends, though underneath she is a driven Gemini at heart.

Her Libra Moon makes her gentle. She has that elusive sweetness with her loved ones and friends, but with a steely masculine strength underneath. Home ties are very important. Because she has a strong Mars in her chart, conjuncting her sun, she is apt to stand up for a principle. This would be understandable based on the two past lives we saw.

If you look further at her chart, the Southern hemisphere, the upper half, which describes a life dealing with the public, is definitely where you find most of her planets. When she became challenged by others around her, in the two previous lives of Hannah and Blue Eyes, she proved her strength through making decisions about these life challenges. In this current life, Martha builds on that strength as seen in her natal chart.

Where Martha's true calling can be found in her chart is where Saturn is located and its ruler. Saturn is retrograde* in her second house. The retrograde tells us that she never learned how to deal with money or the privileges it provides as Hannah in her most recent past life.

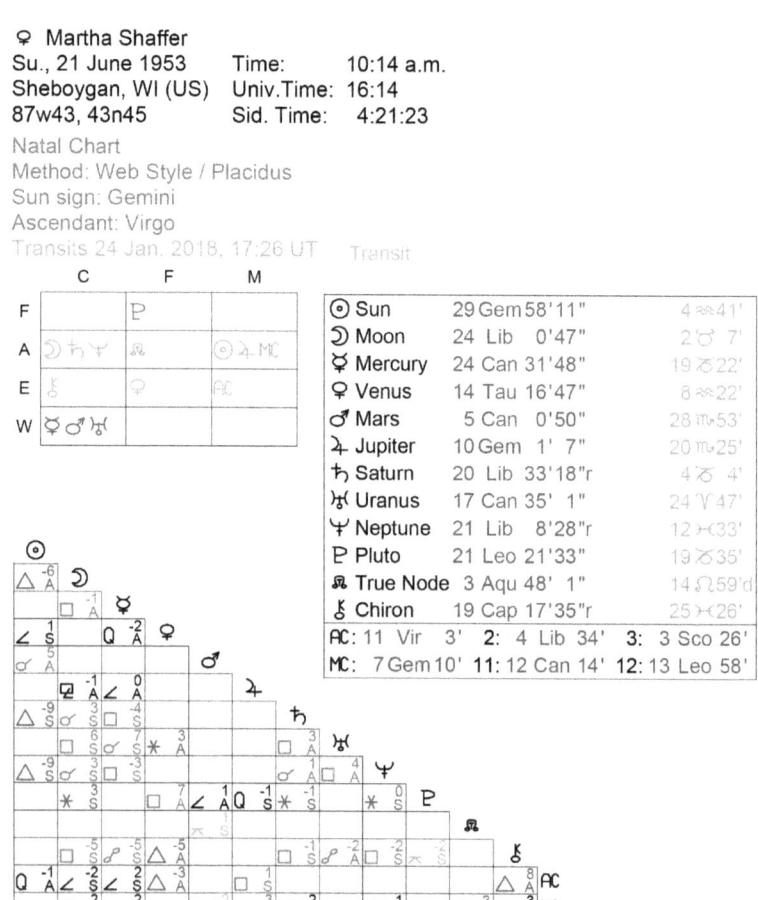

The second house describes how we value money and our possessions. A retrograde to a planet will always show us where our loss of strength can be found. So, her lesson in this life is to learn how to deal with money and to be financially successful. Neptune conjuncting her Saturn makes that point even a little more confusing and blurry. She is many times

*Retrograde: A planet that is Retrograde in a natal chart "appears" to be going backward in movement speed when someone is born. One does not receive the full and active power of the planet.

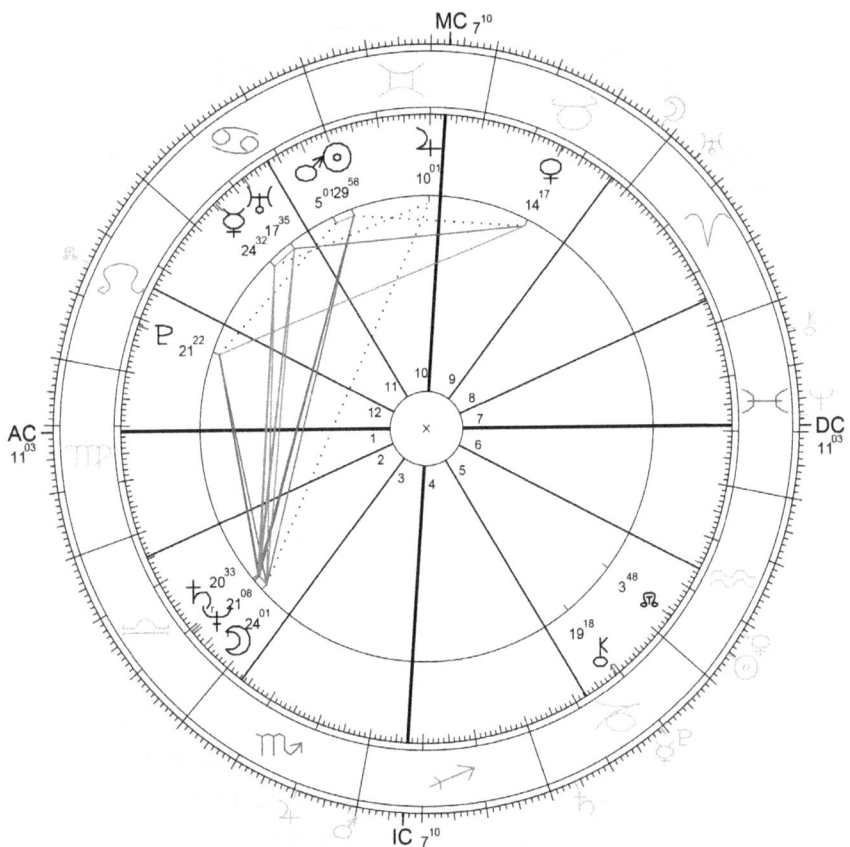

torn between what she must achieve financially to take care of herself, and what she should do for others.

Her Moon in the second house as well, and conjuncting her Saturn, rules her emotional nature and causes her to feel her self-worth is defined by her financial success. This present life is to show her soul what she can achieve on her own, not as a group member of a tribe, as Blue Eyes was, or as a resistance team member as Hannah.

If you look at Capricorn, the ruler of Saturn, it is ruling her fifth house of creativity. The fifth house describes our creativity in all its forms. It could be writing, speaking, singing, even having children. She planned to be creative in her leadership in this life. Capricorn is always practical and manifests what it needs. She would be driven to write, speak, and lead groups in any endeavor she finds herself in, and to follow through in all that she does creatively.

Next, by looking at Chiron and her North Node in the fifth house, we find a driven soul that has gone after the leadership qualities many times in her soul experiences. However, the South Node, being in the opposite eleventh house, tells us she was simply a member of a group in her most recent life, and did not lead. Now with the soul's experience of Blue Eyes and Hannah behind her, she is ready to lead. Through achieving an education in psychology in this lifetime, Martha is here to be a leader, a speaker, and a creator of ideas for others.

The North Node is what Martha came to work on in this life. She came to be a creative leader. To speak, write, and develop methods of learning for others to achieve their goals in life. She is achieving that in many of her endeavors with one-on-one clients. She also is teaching others in her community about Policy Governance, Hospice care, and End-of-Life options. These two past lives gave her the experience to lead with confidence.

Chiron says that she is a responsible soul but needs to learn where to put her energies. Chiron is the wounded healer and shows us what we have been working on for many lives to overcome, not just the ones we witnessed. With Chiron in Capricorn she may feel that she carries the burden or responsibility for other people in their lives, and has difficulty setting boundaries for herself. She is here to learn to let others live their lives, and take the time for Martha personally. Only then, will she excel in her present life. Chiron says this is a challenge for her to overcome in her present life after many lives of service to others.

As we look at the important planets of the Sun, Mars, and Jupiter in her tenth house of career, we see a soul that planned to be a leader of people and groups. Mars conjuncting her Sun gives her the determination to stand her ground and complete her path in leading others through service. She has the experience as a soul, and only when she succeeds at that path will she be completely happy. In addition, with Uranus, the unexpected events planet, and Mercury, the communication planet, in her eleventh house of group, friends, goals and associations, it is very clear where her soul's purpose is.

She is here to be a spokesman for groups and events. She is to use her voice to speak, possibly to unusual or less popular groups, (Uranus), to give them strength. The Hospice and End-of-Life groups are perfect examples of this. The soul of Martha says this time I am going to make a difference, and it is going to have the individual stamp of Martha Shaffer all over it!

Now, to complete our confirmation of Martha's path, we did a psychic tarot card reading for her. The cards that came up for her included the eight of Cups. This card indicates that her old life is behind her, and she is starting to look at a new future. The King of Swords was a prominent card in her spread. This means she has reached the pinnacle of her mind's learning how to lead, and she is ready to use her wisdom.

I asked about her living arrangements. She was renting a home but had a renter to help with the expenses. She said he was leaving soon, and she was concerned about replacing him. The Judgement card, (You will receive your due reward), and the three of Pentacles card, (Skills you have kept hidden are now coming to light), indicated Martha is in a new phase of life and has new skills to meet the economic challenge caused by the departure of her rental.

I then asked about her career in Policy Governance becoming more prominent for her. The cards show much change and imagination with the Knight of Wands. Also the Three of Cups, which means joy, love and financial success, kept coming through for her. That tells me although she will have some challenges, the seven of Wands, she will be able to overcome these challenges, and succeed as an instructor. The seven of Wands also tells me that she may be traveling to other cities in Colorado to teach other school boards or charter school boards on this policy training.

The seven of Pentacles came through for Martha, which means that all her hard work, all her education, and experience were coming back to reward her. When I asked if she should be concerned over finances when the renter left, the cards said she would be seeing new success in her life to cover the changes.

By drawing the Ace of Pentacles, The cards tell me that she is starting on a new, exciting venture, and that money will not be a problem.

In closing, we discussed the fact that her soul chose to come back to earth at critical times in our history. Blues Eyes was here for the end of the freedom that Native Americans knew on the open plains of America. Hannah was a crusader against Facism at a crucial time in Earth's history that no one will ever forget. Now, she has picked a time in our history where we have a new president of the United States, North Korea is threatening the world with bombs, England is pulling out of the Euro dollar, and Russia and the United States are imposing sanctions on each other because of the hacking into emails that Russia did during our election process. Her soul knew she could make a difference at a very vulnerable time for Americans once again. Working with individuals for their mental health, with groups as they decide on cremation and hospice care, and with boards as they solve dilemmas for their organizational systems, Martha can be there to help them make their choices.

Martha's soul is peaking at a time in her 60s when most people slow down their effort in life. She is just beginning her greatest leadership efforts.

Chapter Five

Lee Mitchell
The Hypnotherapist

Many people ask me how I got interested in hypnotherapy. It is a subject I have been fascinated with all my adult life. My first evidence of it that I remember is concerning a motorcycle accident I had on my brother's bike when I was seventeen. Steve was bruised and cut up a little, but I had a big cut on the shine of my left leg. It required over a hundred stitches. I was reading Edgar Cayce books at the time and he had a remedy for the scarring that big cuts can have, and I used it to help heal the scar. Cayce was called the "Sleeping Prophet." He read the future, prescribed remedies for ailments, and saw past lives. All while he was in deep trance, as if he was asleep. Even at seventeen, the past life information he gave out was especially intriguing for me.

I also read the "Seth Speaks" book by Jane Roberts, in my twenties. The first one I read was published in 1972 and is still in publication. I was just graduating from college. I was twenty one, and more and more amazed by what these spiritual intuitives could tell us about past lives. Seth, an advanced being in spirit, actually channeled through Jane, and spoke of knowledge concerning the effect of past lives on our current lives today as well as much, much more.

When Dr. Michael Newton, PhD. came out with his books, "Journey of Souls" in 1994, and "Destiny of Souls" in 2000, I really resonated with his process of hypnotherapy and especially his creation of the "Life Between Lives" sessions he describes in these books. The Life Between Lives sessions involved the client going to a much deeper state, called the Theta Brain Wave State, and visiting many stations in the spirit realm while they are in a soul state. I found it all fascinating. The fascination has never ended for me. Today, I too, do both Past Life Regressions and Between Lives Regressions.

Dr. Brian Weiss introduced his best seller in 1988, "Many Lives, Many Masters". That book brought an increased awareness in past life work to the public more than any before it. I must say that over the years, since I was certified in 2008, by a therapist who trained and taught with Dr. Michael Newton, the growing understanding of the importance of past life study is becoming more and more in demand. My website, www.crystalsoulpath.com, gets inquiries weekly on having a past life session for many, many reasons. I tell people my work is like reading a mystery novel every day. I never know where the client is going to take us, and where we will eventually land.

I find it so interesting to learn about the different parts of our history on Earth, the different types of souls and where they have originated from, and the different dimensions that exist within our very atmosphere, such as the Fairy realm.

All of this information comes from the client in an altered state while tapping into their subconscious mind. I have discovered in all my various cases that many, many people can be changed forever in their present life just by returning to an important past life to process a very important event or relationship that frees them to more fully step into their soul's path today.

But I am a soul living a human life just like the rest of you reading this. I, too, have a soul's path that I came to work on in this present life. This chapter will try to flush out exactly what that is for me.

A colleague was kind enough to read my script so that I could experience the past lives. She did an effective job and I was able to go into the altered state of consciousness just as easily as all my clients do.

In the first scene, I saw myself as a woman in her 30s in England or Scotland in 1675. I knew that her name was Sarah and that she was wearing a draped shawl over her clothes with a hood to hide her head. She had on homemade leather shoes. Sarah's dress was plaid and it was below her knees with long sleeves. I saw my face as having a large nose with a mole on it. My hair was in a bun.

The next scene finds me older and I am on my way home. My home is a little cottage with a thatched roof. It has log walls. I live alone. I do have a cat named Katy that I recognized as the soul essence of my beloved dog, Casey, who passed in 2016 at age 16. I see that I had a teacher who taught me of herbs, healing light, and remedies for healing. The soul essence of the teacher I see is my Grandmother, Lillie, in my present life. My

Grandmother, Lillie, was also a mentor for me in my present life, as Lee. She passed when I was 19, yet she taught me how to be strong and independent.

In the next scene I see that I am much older and starting to be hunched over. I am closely connected to a businessman in the town. Our town was very small and made up of farmers mostly. My friend's name is Thomas. I recognize his soul essence as that of a banker friend in my current life, Carl Charette, who I met in Salida, Colorado in 1999.

This friend, Thomas, was my closest friend, and advised me on my life as I became the healer for this little town. I grew my own herbs, and made liquid potions from them. As an herbalist, I also used my ability to transfer healing light to customers to help them heal their bodies.

I did not want anyone to know my talents for healing. I feared I would suffer repercussions from authorities, if they knew of my healing practices. Many would call me a witch or a sage. Yet, I started to teach other young woman in the area in small, secret gatherings at my place. I passed down all I knew to the young women by the time I was in my 60s.

I see that I passed peacefully around age 75. I thanked the soul of Thomas for being there as a dear friend for me all my life. Then I felt my soul lifting out of Sarah's body.

When my colleague asked me to explain my soul's path in that prior life, my higher consciousness told me it was to learn to be of service in all that I do. I believe I accomplished that as Sarah, the healer and teacher.

My next life was as a young man named Robert in the early 1800s. I lived with my grandfather who owned a ranch. He shared the ranch with my father and mother who lived in another house on the ranch. I grew up with him, though I knew my parents were close by. The ranch eventually turned into a milk producing business. We were one of the first families that bottled the milk for delivery to stores and customers.

As I matured, I married Jane who I saw was the soul essence of Dan, my partner today and the love of my life. We had two children. The boy was named Jude and was the soul essence of my brother, Lewis, in my present life. The girl was named Amy, and was the soul essence of my sister, Joanne, today. I saw that my grandfather, in this past life, was the soul essence of my Uncle Johnny in my present life. My Uncle Johnny passed away when I was a young adult growing up in Texas. I always had a special relationship with him, and now I understand why.

Robert was somewhere in the Midwest in this past life. It felt like Missouri or Kansas. My big family led a humble life. We were hard-working ranchers, raising chickens as well as growing a big garden of corn and wheat for the cows. We packaged milk and butter for the area stores.

As I became older, I pulled away from the family business and opened a small lumber mill with a local general store. I saw myself at age 65 with white hair and mustache. I was happy and content. My wife was still alive and our daughter was married with children of her own. Our son had taken over the lumber business by then.

At age 73, I saw myself weak and ready to leave this life. I felt that my wife, Jane, had always been a wonderful partner.

She was loving and caring. We respected each other and allowed each other to grow in that life. I hated to leave her.

As I left that life, I was asked again what was my soul's path as Robert. I distinctly felt it was to support the family, my parents, my grandfather, my wife and children. We were all a team that fully shared in the responsibilities of a family run business. It was a rewarding life.

This is a very different experience than my current life where I am not particularly close to my family and moved away from my siblings when I was in my 20s. My mother died when I was fourteen and my parents divorced when I was four, and I never had a relationship with my father. I believe the guides wanted me to understand that I had planned this independent life to do my work, yet I had, in past lives, experienced warm and close family relationships with some of the same souls who are in my life today.

Several of my spirit guides came through that day as well. Aranthia, my master guide, was the first to come through to communicate with me. I see him as very tall and wearing a white robe, (I call it the Jesus outfit). I see that he has reddish brown hair and a beard. Johnathan is another very familiar guide. He has been a human in past lives with me, but in this present life, he is one of my main guides. He appears as a Greek man about 40 years old. He has black curly hair and is fairly short, maybe 5'8". I also saw my grandmother, Lillie, and immediately felt warm inside. We had a wonderful relationship in this life until she passed. I feel her presence around me often, as I do my guides. Finally, many of my furry children who have passed came through. I saw Nikia, Tasha, Frazier, and Casey. They are just some of my dogs that have passed. I even saw Zebe, my stripped cat.

Their message for me was to be kinder and gentler when with Dan, my partner. I expect a lot from him in this life. There is an unconscious feeling of trust between us. I now understand that we have had several lives together in the past that has allowed our bond to build over many, many experiences. Today, we continue to build on that trust and companionship as never before.

The first scene of this third past life was a scene that was not connected to the rest of the life, but it was important for me to feel and see. I see myself walking into a dark, thick forest. I am 12 years old and my name is Linda. The year is 1941. What was so crucial for me to remember was what I felt next. I felt the energies of witches, or healers, in this forest in hiding. I couldn't see them, but I could clearly feel their presence.

The next scene showed me and my family back in America. My father was in the military, and we had been stationed in Germany. The dark, thick forest had been in Germany. Now back home, I see myself in the backyard playing with my brother. His name is Donald. I see him as the soul essence of my Uncle Johnny in my present life. I also have an older sister. I do not recognize her soul essence as anyone I know today. I appear to be very happy.

The next scene moves me to a scene where I am now 18 years old. I am in the same house. I see that I have on bobby sox and a mid-calf length "Poodle skirt." That was a type of skirt that was full circle skirt with petticoats underneath. They were popular during the late 50s and early 60s. I see that I start college for an Engineering degree. Next I see that I am married and my husband is a college professor. I later become a college professor, as well, who taught Engineering. I recognize my husband as the soul essence of a boy I dated in high school in my present life named Johnny Button. I remember that he and I had a somewhat boring relationship in high school. And I feel the same situation happened to Linda and her husband's relationship. We just worked and lived a very sedate life. We stayed in one place all our lives. I see that we had two children.

I see that I passed at 78 years old. This would be an overlapping parallel life with my current one as Lee. Linda died in 2007. I was born in 1949, and Linda was born in 1929. I was experiencing an overlapping parallel life with my current one.

Parallel overlapping lives are fairly common with our advanced soul lives today. About ten percent of my cases involve parallel lives. We choose to overlap two different lives several decades or more apart. There are many reasons for this. The number one reason is to grow our souls faster. We do split our soul's energy into two humans for many years, and that does affect our stamina as a human. But we are willing to do that because we can experience and grow as a soul twice as fast that way.

Also, I find in some cases, the soul decides to enter into an additional life in a certain time and place to complete a soul commitment with other souls in their soul group. The soul must split its energy in the second parallel life to be in that generation at a certain time and place to complete the contract. We, as souls, do this from a higher consciousness with no regret of spreading our energy very thin.

Usually the year the parallel life passes away, the remaining human still incarnated with the same soul will experience a huge shift and possibly start on a new path. For me, in 2007, I moved from Crestone, Colorado to Salida, Colorado with my general contracting and real estate business. In Salida, I began the shift into Past Life Regression therapy and psychic intuitive readings away from real estate. It was a big change that I had thought about for decades. The new energy that came to me, because my parallel life as Linda had ended, helped me finally make the shift.

I also believe that the soul of Linda wanted me to be a risk taker because she had not been. She wanted more from life, and I was going to make that happen for her as well as for me.

The soul's path for Linda had been to be stable and follow through with her teaching plans. She did that, and fulfilled my soul's desire to start something and stay until the end. She completed a detailed life as a college professor. Funny, in this present life, I have only had one male friend that was a college professor. I remember thinking how foreign it was to my way of thinking of being a risk taker. It was a reminder to my soul not to get off the task of going into the hypnotherapy path to help others.

The last experience I viewed of a past life was as a male. My name was Jedidiah. I see the first scene as Jedidiah when he was 18. I lived on a farm with my parents. The first scene was of me climbing over a wooden fence, and walking up to a red painted barn. I have blonde hair, and I am very tall. I see that my father is dark skinned and has dark hair. I believe he is my step-father. My mother's first marriage ended quickly after I was born, and she remarried. I didn't like him much. He's very rough and stern. Next, I see that he is repairing some farm equipment, and he wants me to help. I know that he wants me to just work with him all the time on the farm. But, I want to go to town, and do other things with my life. It is 1848, and I know that I am in the West. I feel we are in Wyoming. My Mom is light haired and very kind. She is much younger than my Step-Dad. I see that the Step-Dad is the soul essence of my brother-in-law, Wayne, in my present life. I did not like my brother-in-law, Wayne, in my current life. He was a big drinker in my present life. He died from a heart attack in his late 50s.

I have a sister as well. She is the soul essence of my best friend from high school in my present life, Robin Fitch. As I turned twenty-two, I see that I am dating a young woman of eighteen named Marla. I know that we marry soon after that scene. I see that she is the soul essence of Dan, my partner today. I see us on a horse and buggy going to town. I can see that she is very beautiful. She has a smooth complexion and dark black hair and eyebrows. Soon, I begin working at a bank in town. I eventually work my way up to the Mayor of the town! Marla and I have two children. The boy is the soul essence of my brother today, Steve. Steve passed away in my present life at age 40. I always felt very protective of him. The girl was named Erica. I do not recognize her soul essence as anyone in my present life.

I need to break for a moment and explain soul groups. When anyone sees someone in a past life during a session, I always stop and ask them if they recognize the soul as anyone they know in their current life today. They may not be the same sex or look the same as they do today, but we immediately "feel" who they are to us today. About 75% of the time, the client will tell me it is someone they are related to, work with, or friend in their current life. These are members of our soul groups. They are souls who have contracts with us. We commit to planned associations with these same group of souls, life after life, in order to grow our soul through intimate experiences and relationships.

Let's return to Jedidiah's past life. As I saw myself age, I noted that I had white hair and a white mustache. However, I become a workaholic, and never seem to slow down. I see that I pass at 68 from a heart attack as I walk down the street of the town. I was always trying to help the community members of our little town, and I didn't take care of my health. I left this little town too soon. This was a clear message to me from my higher consciousness. I have been guilty of putting work first, and my personal life second in my present life. I see that my wife, (Dan), continues to carry on without me. As I worked very hard as Mayor of our little town, she became very involved in volunteer work, and continued volunteering after I left.

My guides are quickly all around me as I pass as Jedidiah. I see Aranthia, Johnthan, Marcy, Simon, Loneagle, and Filamenta, an angel who guides me. They tell me, out of the blue, to not be worried about our new Rhodesian Ridgeback rescue dog, Toby. They tell me he is going to be a great dog. His soul essence is part of Starsky, one of Dan's dog's that has passed, and part of Nikia, my female Rhodesian Ridgeback, who passed when she was nine in 2009.

My guides tell me that the reason they showed me these two past lives that day was to remind me that I didn't want a predictable, stable life like Linda's parallel life had been. In addition, I am aware of being a workaholic, in my present life. As I have aged, I have set the intention to find time to play, travel, and enjoy the beauty of my home and yard as well as enjoy my professional work. My guides were reminding me that it's not all work, and no play, like Jedidiah's life became. One major theme for my present life is "balance".

The first two lives, I had requested. The last two were just a bonus that my friend volunteered to do when we had a second session. Concerning the first session I had, I had always wondered if I had had a past life as a healer, and my guides were kind enough to show me the life as Sarah, the healer in 1675. I had wondered where I gained this confidence to do the work I do, and it is from Sarah's life. The second past life was to show me I have experienced very close family ties with others as opposed to my present life.

I live a solidary life today to do my work of service, much like Sarah. But I chose this as a soul. I wanted this independent life to be strong enough to do the emotional work it requires to meet with clients and unearth their deepest wounds. Much was learned and processed in these sessions for me. I also learned that Dan had been with me twice as my partner. I have also seen him in another past life where he was a man in 1799 that was a mature, successful businessman in Scotland. You will read more about him in his session. We were close in that life as well, but we never married. I feel the same kindness from Dan today as I felt from my wife, Jane, and my wife, Darla, in those two past lives. We are clearly here together to forward our growth as souls and help each other in many ways.

Now we are on to my Astrological Natal chart. In the chart attached, my Sun is in Sagittarius, my rising sign is Libra, and my moon is in Aquarius. My "Skeleton" describes a person who likes freedom. As they age, Sagittarius's become much more spiritual. My Libra rising sign would show someone that appears very pleasant and receptive on the outside, but with a steel determination to achieve underneath. My Moon in Aquarius would show that I do not demonstrate a great deal of emotion in one-on-one relationships. However, Aquarius moon, is a fixed sign, and is a dependable and loving partner. This is a trait of Aquarians whether they know it or not. Aquarius Moon means I am very loyal to my friends and family as well.

We look to the North and South node to understand the lessons of the most recent past life, and what I am working on in my current life. The North node is in my seventh house of partnerships. I planned on working with partners (clients) very closely, as well as romantic and business partners. I have been married three times and have seen all my husbands in past lives. We all came to complete contracts we had in other lives.

For example, I have seen a past life with my last husband, Doug Mitchell, in a Native American life together. In it, he was the chief of our tribe, and I was the young warrior training under him. When he passed, I took over to lead the tribe. But in battle, I saw that I made a poor choice in strategy, and got most of my warriors killed.

I see now that as Doug's soul came through in this life as my husband, he mainly connected with me to help me make the decision to come to Colorado. My spiritual path awakened after I moved to Colorado in 1999. For after only four years we decided to divorce, as I had made the decision to move to Colorado from Florida and he chose to stay in Florida. He was still being my mentor to help me see my path, just as he had been as my chief all those years ago.

Later, in Colorado, I realized that that had been our contract. He was here to help me become the professional with my own business who would work with clients, both in home-building and in hypnotherapy. North node in seventh house of partnerships is exemplified by this contract with Doug. Partners in this life are to be very important to me whether they be personal or business ones.

The one-on-one past life and between life regression sessions are very intimate relationships where clients are telling me their worst fears, their worst traumas, and much

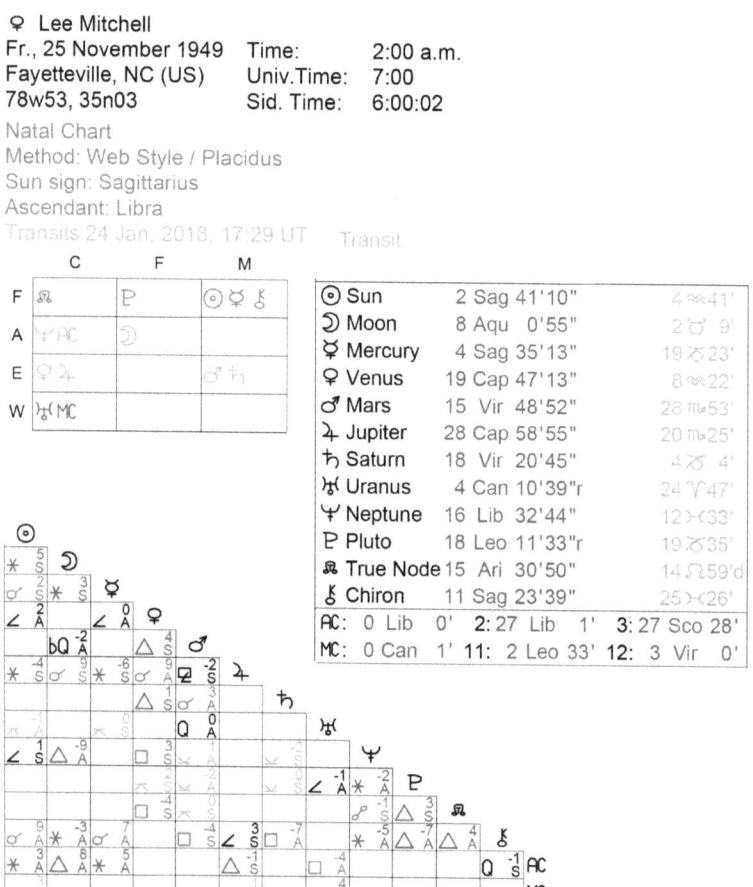

more. This was to be my path. I am to be independent in my work but to build very important working relationships with others in service to them.

The South node is automatically in my first house based on the North node being in my seventh house. It is always in the opposite house from the North node placement. This lets you know where you came from in your most recent past life. I have seen this past life, and I was a maid in England trying to move away from family. I stretched myself to make a living on my own. I later lived on the streets when I was too old to be a

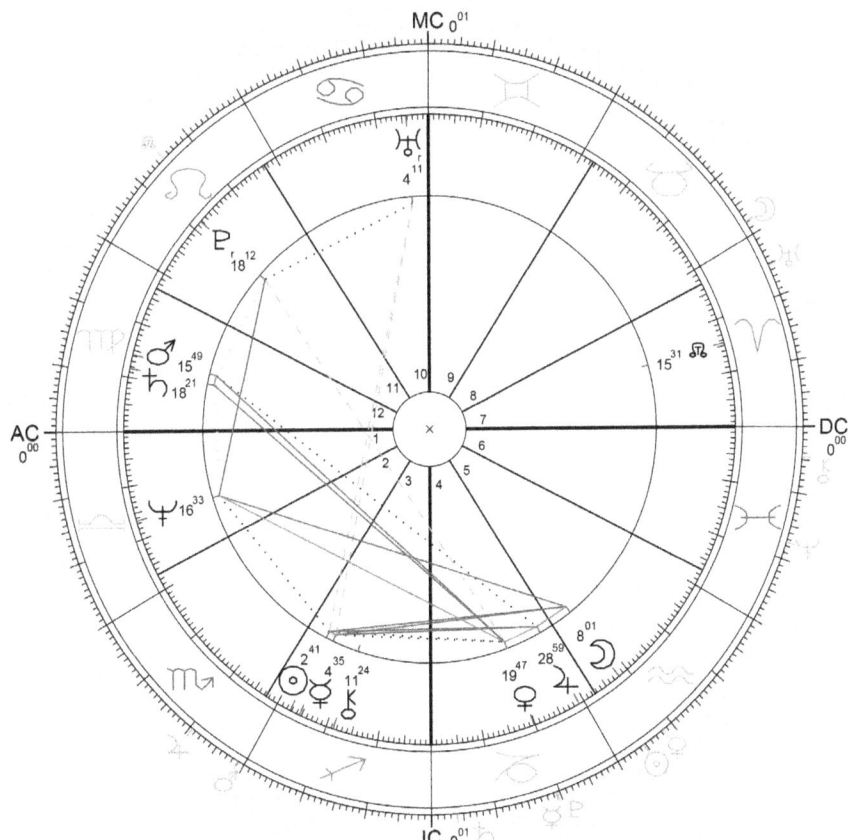

maid as a senior citizen. I was helped by the soup kitchens who fed me regularly. What I was doing was a dress rehearsal for my present life. I was being very self-centered as I tried to live an independent life. Yet, I was still very dependent on others for my well-being by having my South node in Libra, the ruler of my first house. I was trying to discover a life of balance, which is a major theme of Libra's. This most recent past life was preparing me for my present life of being very independent with my own business, only after being of service and working for other people in my most recent past life.

Saturn is also an indicator of present life paths based on the experiences you learned in your most recent past life. My Saturn is in my twelfth house. This would describe a need to move beyond a selfish attitude to one of service. I must serve or I will suffer in my present life.

The ruler of Saturn, Capricorn, is also an indicator of past life and present life paths. Capricorn rules my fifth house of creativity, children, and romance. Capricorn is a practical earth sign. I will show my creativity through practical ways. Even hypnotherapy is a very practical science of tapping into the subconscious mind. In romance, I must give in order to receive. Once again, the selfish tendency pops up. In this life, yes, I can be independent, but I must not forget to be of service and give back in all I do. This is to balance the most previous life of aloneness and self-interest. An important principal point to make is that the soul will naturally balance itself from life to life. It becomes aware it is getting off center from a previous life, and will pick a life that brings itself challenges to achieve balance once more.

Chiron, our last indicator is in my third house. As I search for my individuality and personal freedom, I have come to explore my spirituality because Chiron is in my third house ruled by Sagittarius. Sagittarius energy is always searching for the meaning in life, and personal growth through the study of spirituality. My fear, with the wound of Chiron here, is that I will find that I am insignificant and unworthy as a soul. Therefore, my battle with this life is to have faith, step out and take risks. I am to discover the ultimate truth that we are truly all integral and essential parts of creation. The career I have grown into requires many risks and leaps of faith to achieve.

I have Neptune in my first house ruled by Libra. Many spiritual people and intuitives have Neptune placed here. Even religious soul paths will find Neptune placed here. One's presence among others will always be focused on the higher dimensions of our existence when you have Neptune in the first house. I also have Uranus in my tenth house of public career. Uranus gives strength to the unusual and unexpected. When placed here, it means that I will always delve into unusual careers. My first career as real estate broker and developer was somewhat unusual for a woman. And of course, the path I have taken as a Past Life Regression therapist is considered an unusual life path.

My Sun and my Mercury placed in the third house of communication denotes that I will succeed in whatever I do by the use of communication. Through speaking, writing, teaching and social media, I will be of service.

Finally, by having my Saturn and Mars in the twelfth house of buried issues, I have found my soul's emphasis. I hold my Mars energy back through the use of the groundedness of Saturn. Saturn is the teacher of lessons. Unless, I serve others, I will not experience the reward of my Mars energy in any kind of lasting success.

Turning to my Tarot Card spread, we find similar issues brought through. I received cards such as four of Swords that express my sense of pushing too hard in my daily activities. I also received the two of Swords which tells me that I am undecided presently on what to give up to lighten my load. I want to respond to clients and help with their needs. I also want to spend personal time with Dan and our dog, Toby, doing leisurely activities that I enjoy. Using the Celtic Cross spread, I next received the five of Wands. This indicates the frustration over how to balance the two parts of my life. We know that I came to find my path of service, yet learn how to balance my life in personal relationships as well.

The "head" card of the Celtic Cross spread, the fifth card in the spread, is the Justice card. This means that I feel it is my due reward to enjoy my leisure time more. I have worked hard, and it is time.

The ten of Pentacles in my spread indicates that much good fortune financially is coming to me. This means that all my efforts will pay off for me toward my financial security, as I go forward. My work has been appreciated, and many returns will come to me.

I also received the ten of Cups which describes the relationship I have with Dan, my partner. I feel fully supported in my work by him, and he is my rock that I lean on after a busy day of session work with clients. The next card, the two of Cups, confirms that we are building a bond that promotes close friendship. I can tell him all my deepest secrets, and he the same with me. This is a great thing to discover so late in life.

Finally, the end result card is the Queen of Wands which is my card. Whenever I read for myself, I always receive this card.

It describes a woman of action, never sitting still, and a multi-tasker. My task is to accomplish much for others in service, and to balance it with a loving relationship with Dan. This is a mutual goal we both have addressed together in previous lives.

I treasure this information for my future. It enlightens me as never before. It sheds new light on this ever changing life, and I look forward to the future and what it may hold for both of us.

Chapter Six

Dan Ely

The Compassionate Finance Manager

Dan Ely and I met over two years ago. I know him as a kind, generous, loving father and grandfather who just wants to live his life to be happy and enjoy each day. We met through Match.com. He was recently divorced from a twenty year marriage, and I was also divorced but had been single for over eighteen years. We met for breakfast one Sunday. and never stopped dating. A few months later, since both of us were renting our home, we decided to buy a house together. Many people would say that we had not given ourselves enough time to know each other very well. We had not even lived together, only spending a few days each week together.

Here is where the past life regression sessions can really help a person understand their relationships. Many of us have simply chosen this present life to work on evolving personal relationships with members of our soul group. I had a chance to trade regression sessions with another hypnotherapist shortly after Dan and I met. Of course, my burning question was had I had a past life with Dan. The life I was shown was from 1799 in Scotland. I was a school teacher, and Dan was an affluent businessman somewhat older than I. I would not marry him, when he asked, because I truly enjoyed my teaching career. In those times, women married to prominent men did not work. They volunteered and/or raised the children. I saw that many of my friends were bored with their station in life. So, our entire lives were spent dating, but not being together.

I am sure we did not even spend the night together. There were not Motel 6s or Super Eights at that time. Plus a woman would never sleep over at a man's home in 1799. Fast forward to the present, and this past life regression helped me to understand why we connected so quickly, and why we decided to buy a home together so quickly. It was to catch up on so many days we had missed being together in that past life in Scotland. I immediately trusted Dan. That is another clue to a soul contract. You usually feel very comfortable with the other person, and feel as if you have known them before. That is because your souls recognize each other. It is meant to be that way during a human incarnation so that we will not pass by the other person easily, and miss the contract we came to complete.

As we investigate his past lives, we are both curious if we will indeed discover more that we have shared together in personal, intimate relationships. Dan's higher-self will show him the most crucial experiences he needs to visit once again, in order to free him from any trauma he may be bringing forward into his current life in order to release it once and for all.

As we begin his session, Dan sees that there are bars on the door. It slides open and shut, he says. It does not need a door knob. He sees two spirit guides opening the door in front of him. Inside the structure, he sees picnic tables and people. He also sees shower stalls and more doors. He is wearing sandals and an orange jumpsuit. He tells me his name is Rick, and he is in Arizona. The year is 1938. Rick is in prison, Dan tells me.

Rick was sentenced to prison for killing a stranger. This stranger had killed his brother. His brother was stabbed to death as the killer was robbing him. The thief was not planning on getting caught. But Rick arrived late for his appointment with his brother, and the killer was still there. When he saw that the killer had stabbed and killed his brother, Rick was so enraged that he began to beat him up. The beating was so severe that it killed the man. Rick was in his thirties when he was sentenced to prison for the killing, Dan said.

In the next scene, Dan sees that Rick is now getting out of jail. Dan tells me that he sees Rick has a personal bag with him, and he is getting on a bus. He is going back home to see his Mom. When he gets to his Mom's house in his home town, no one is there. He asked the neighbor where his Mother was, and she tells him his mother had recently died. Next, Dan sees Rick at the cemetery looking for his mother's grave. He finds her grave. The year she died was the present year. His Mother never knew where Rick was all those years while he was in prison. His Mother was the only parent he had ever known. He had never met his Father. He now had nowhere to go.

In the next scene, Dan sees that Rick is in a single room. Rick is now working at a school as a janitor. He is in his 50s now, Dan tells me. He is still in his hometown. Rick is just living each day as simply as he can. He regrets he did not see his Mom one more time before she passed away. She was in her 80s, and was very old and feeble. Rick feels very guilty for his actions, and wishes he had made better choices.

I asked Dan to move to a later time in Rick's life. He sees him still working at the school. Rick is now sixty-six years old. The year is 1948. Rick feels okay, Dan says. He has had no relationships. But Rick tells himself it is the right thing to do to stay here, and work out his last days.

On his last day, Dan sees that Rick is still in his single room. He is tired and ready to go. Dan says Rick appeared to die in his sleep. He is 72 years old. He passed in 1954. As I asked if there was a family member he would like to say goodbye to, Dan asked for Rick's mother and brother to come through. He told his mother how sorry he was that he missed her. She told him it was okay, but that she never knew where he was. Dan did not recognize the soul of his mother as anyone he knows in his present life.

Next, he asked to say goodbye to Rick's brother. Dan told me that he saw that his brother had a wife and two kids that he left behind when he was murdered. Rick felt so sorry that he had not gotten there earlier that night. His brother said that it was okay. We calculated the birthday of Dan, and we realized that this was a brief, overlapping parallel life. Dan was born in 1952. Therefore, he was only two years old when Rick passed. The higher-self of Dan had already started his life as Dan before the end of Rick's. Probably he could see that Rick was not moving forward in his life at that point.

In leaving that life, I asked Dan what his soul's path had been. He told me that he was supposed to protect his Mother and his brother in that lifetime. He said he did not accomplish either of those missions.

In knowing Dan today, he appears to be there for all his family. His Mother and Father have passed, but he was always connected to his Mother to help her in any way. He has three siblings, and he has always been the older brother they call on whenever they need help. He is unusually determined to help them in any way. Any feeling of guilt from Dan's past life has been counterbalanced in his current life by his active commitment to his family.

In the second past life, Dan sees that he is outside on a ridge. He sees water behind him and a tree down below the ridge. Over the ridge, he sees a house. I asked if Dan would go to the house and simply walk inside. He does that, and he sees that everything is wood inside. The furniture, the walls, the floor are all wood. The house is one big room. There is no fireplace. He sees a family there. I asked if the family was his, and Dan says. "Yes." He has a wife named Jean, he says. His name is Bob. He sees that he has three children all under the age of twelve. He says he does not recognize the soul of any of his family members. Dan tells me that Bob is in his thirties. They are in Northwest Oregon. The year is 1911. He is a rancher and he has cows and chickens. He is very happy, Dan says. He comments that the countryside is beautiful.

As we move forward in Bob's life, Dan sees that he is in his 40s now, and still working the ranch. The children are helping him. His oldest daughter is getting married. I asked Dan if he recognized the soul energy of the future husband, and he said he did not recognize him as anyone he knew in his present life. He sees that his wife is busily planning the wedding.

Still in his 40s now, Bob sees that his daughter is now married, and she has moved away with her new husband. Dan sees that Bob is fishing with his son at the creek. The scene is beautiful. Dan feels that Bob's life is beautiful as well.

As I asked Dan to move Bob to a later time in his life, he sees him sitting in the cabin in his 50s. He is reflecting. The children are all grown and have moved away. But Bob is happy and still enjoys being on the ranch. The kids do come and visit him often. He and his wife are busy taking care of the animals and the vegetables they grow. He continues to fish as well. He likes his life and enjoys every minute.

When we look in on Bob on his last day, Dan sees that he is lying at his beloved creek. He is just tired and ready to go. He simply slips away at the creek. He probably had a heart attack and went quickly. He is 67 years old. When we calculate his birth year and add 67 to it, we discover he passed in 1946. This was Dan's most previous past life.

Rick and Bob had overlapping parallel lives for much of their lives. Dan's higher self is showing him that both these lives are affecting his present life for different reasons. Rick's life is about ambitions not fulfilled and guilt over not having protected his loved ones. And Bob's life reminds Dan how he loves creeks and big Redwood trees, much like the environment he grew up in in California. But now we know that the life of Bob was drawing Dan to those areas. He was very happy as the family man in that previous life, and he was being drawn back to that similar area to relive the feeling of joy and contentment Bob had in Oregon.

A return to the most previous life or overlapping parallel lives, as in Dan's case, is not a common client experience. Only if there is something or someone from the past life or lives that is affecting the client's present life will our guides and higher-self choose to reveal the details of our most recent past lives. Since I know Dan personally, I can tell you he grew up in Southern California, but visited Grandparents in Northern California where he got to enjoy the outdoors and fishing. Much of Northern California terrain is similar to Oregon. He has commented many times that he so loved growing up around the little creeks with his siblings. They played and fished in those creeks often. He much preferred that to the roaring ocean waves of the Pacific Ocean. After the regressions, I can now appreciate why he so loves those little creeks and the trees around them. He was trying to recreate the life of Bob that so fulfilled him as a soul.

When I asked if there was any member of his family he would like to say goodbye to, Dan said he would like to say goodbye to all of his family. As he brought them through, they all said the same thing. "We love you and miss you." He said, "Ditto."

I asked Dan to reflect on his soul's path in this most recent past life, and he said it was to be happy and in love. He said he definitely completed both of those desires. What a wonderful life!

As Dan's Master Guide came through next, he notes that it is not the same guide he had met in a previous session we had. His name is Preston. He is compassionate and masculine. He is in his 70s with white hair. He has on a shirt and pants, and has a funny goatee. It is really long, Dan said.

Dan reports that his original guide, Torrey, who is female, is also here. He met her in a previous past life session we had.

She has short, short hair, he says. She is very religious. She was in a religious life with him as a human, and now is one of his guides, she tells Dan.

We asked Preston to help us understand why Dan was shown these two particular past lives. Preston says that Dan needs to let the pain of Rick's life go. "Let go and remember Bob's happy life", Preston says. Preston went on to say that Dan should live the life of Bob today. Let go of the sadness of Rick's life. It was to learn responsibility, and you have certainly learned that life lesson in your present life as Dan. Preston says, "let go, and be happy"!

In Dan's present life he has been very responsible. He has three sons, one adopted. The oldest boy was from a high school romance and the couple never married. The other unions ended in divorce, yet he spent time raising the sons and being responsible for their well-being. Today, he has grandchildren and stays in touch with each and every one of them.

I did an attachment release on Dan, after asking Preston if it would help him. I asked his guides to join us, as I call in several of my guides as well. I use the Christ Consciousness light to swirl all around his body and then using my energy, I cut the silver cord that is still attached to Rick. That frees that attachment to Rick, but I go further and send the soul part that was Rick to the "Central Sun" where that part of his soul can be cleansed and renewed. His guides and mine then return that soul-part now renewed and refreshed to join Dan on the sofa, and it is absorbed internally into him. The renewed part of his soul joins the rest of his soul in his body. I then asked Preston if the procedure had helped Dan to release the pain of Rick's guilt. Preston said, "Yes."

I asked Preston what Dan and my contract in his present life was. He said to love and enjoy happiness together. When I asked why it had taken so long to meet up in this life, (We are both in our 60s), Preston had wise words for us. He told us that we both had had to learn how to love. Myself being the workaholic in past lives, and Dan carrying around guilt of not being responsible from Rick's life had made both of us forget the importance of love and happiness. Now we can appreciate the benefits of learning to love together. What a big contract we had asked of ourselves to complete.

Now we move to important insight of Dan's soul path by investigating his Astrological Natal Chart. Dan has his Sun in Libra, his Moon in Gemini, and his Ascendent is in Pisces. Attached you will see Dan's birth chart. Libras are people who have come into this life to find balance with their paths. Maybe in the past this was not accomplished by Dan's soul. Libras see all sides to a dilemma.

Dan is a Purchasing and Logistics manager for a Not-for-Profit Association of Medical Walk-In Clinics. He is in a position to ensure the organization has the proper tools available for the medical staff to care for the low income and indigent people in the community.

If a Clinic needs supplies, he sees that their needs are met. Libras are also very hard working and usually have high expectations for themselves. His Moon being in Gemini would describe a man that is versatile and critical. He can be restless in search for the truth. He has a longing for knowledge. With his Moon in his third house, Dan has an emotional type of mind. Sensitive and imaginative, he absorbs through listening, not book study. He is there to solve the problems of the staff as well as the senior executives through his purchases of supplies for the staff, and the bigger items like sonogram machines, x-ray machines, and more for the senior executives as they open new locations.

As a soul with an Ascendent in Pisces, he is easy-going. In addition, he is sympathetic, supersensitive, and affectionate to others. He is sentimental and extremely psychic. But he can be secretive and impractical at times, as well. Dan is a romantic and a dreamer at times. Spending time alone can be an absolute necessity to process his ideas.

As we look at his indicators for understanding his most recent past life, and what his soul's path is in his present life, Dan's chart is quite forceful in its aim. His Saturn is in his seventh house of partnerships in the sign of Libra, and conjuncting his Sun. He came into this life to work on relationships, but with restraints. When you have Saturn conjuncting the Sun, you hold the full ambitions of the Sun being held down by the restraint of Saturn, the teacher of lessons. Plus, Saturn in the seventh house tells us that his soul had a fear that relationships would restrict him or become burdensome. Early on he did avoid marriage. He had a son by a girlfriend in his early twenties, but they choose never to marry. Dan was a Pro Baseball player and had to travel for his work much of the time. She went on to marry someone else. He did keep connected to the son. Saturn in this placement may have you marry for security reasons later. Dan did go on to marry and have a son of his own again. There was not the deep love between them, but he achieved his purpose which was the start of the security he yearned for from his life as Bob. However, what starts as security may end up being a trap, because many times the partner may have deep insecurities.

Looking at the ruler of Saturn, Capricorn, we learn more. Capricorn rules his eleventh house of goals, friendships and groups. Capricorns are the hardest working earth sign in the zodiac. He would make a good speaker to groups, would be a very loyal friend, and would be aggressive to achieve his goals in life. Reflecting back on his most recent past lives, these traits would help correct the feeling of guilt he had when he was Rick. He did not follow through with helping his brother, and failed to connect with his mother before she died. He also stopped achieving any goals for himself, and instead simply played out his days as a janitor of a school. Rick had a very mild ambition for being such an old soul. His chart says that in this life he plans on changing that experience to one of follow through and dependability. These are traits of a Capricorn.

Rick did not want to face up to responsibility in life after his tragedy in prison. But the longing for the life of happiness that Bob experienced in Oregon, made Dan push for security later in life. He wanted to repeat that dream life with a wife and children in his present life. However, his wife's insecurities ended that wish. After a series of family deaths, she fell into depression and alcohol dependency. They ended their marriage. I met Dan several months later after he had entered therapy to move forward after the divorce.

Next, let's look at the placement of Chiron in Dan's chart. It is in the sign of Capricorn in the tenth house. The tenth house is the house of career, and how one is perceived in that career to the outside world. This tells us that Dan's soul feels tremendous responsibility for helping other people. Remember Chiron is the wounded healer and wherever it is placed we are trying to overcome pain we have suffered.

The major thread that Dan be responsible for others is a recurring theme that has been developed over many lifetimes. His soul has experienced this feeling other times in past lives previous to these we experienced in this session. In addition to the lives we discussed, another past life that Dan experienced in a previous session with me was as a Sheriff in a western town in the 1800s. In that life he lost his daughter to accidental crossfire from a rifle of an angry villain getting revenge on Dan who had arrested him and sent him to jail earlier.

Chiron in the tenth house tell us that he is here to be dependable to others and to always help loved ones in any way

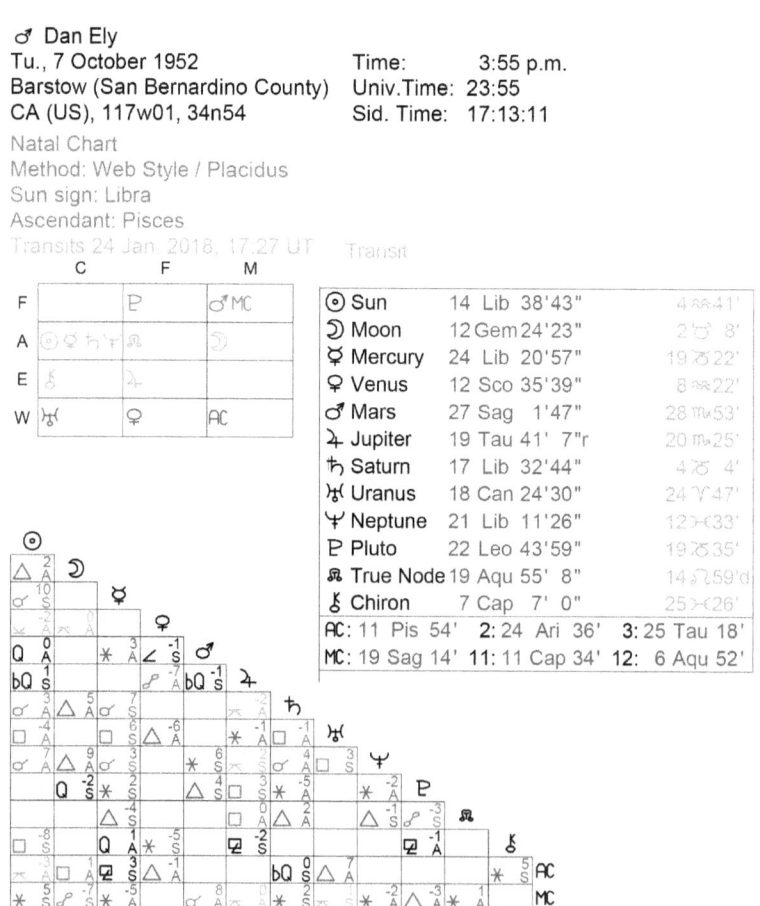

he can. However, Chiron reminds him that the challenge is to learn when to say no. He is here to learn when to walk away from a situation and let the other person work it out for himself. Here is the case for balance again. He may feel he has to save everyone from danger because of his past life experiences. Dan is here to learn when to step up to the challenge of a call to duty, and when to learn to let the other person make their own choices.

Dan's North and South Moon Nodes are in the 12th and 6th houses respectively. The 12th house concerns itself with

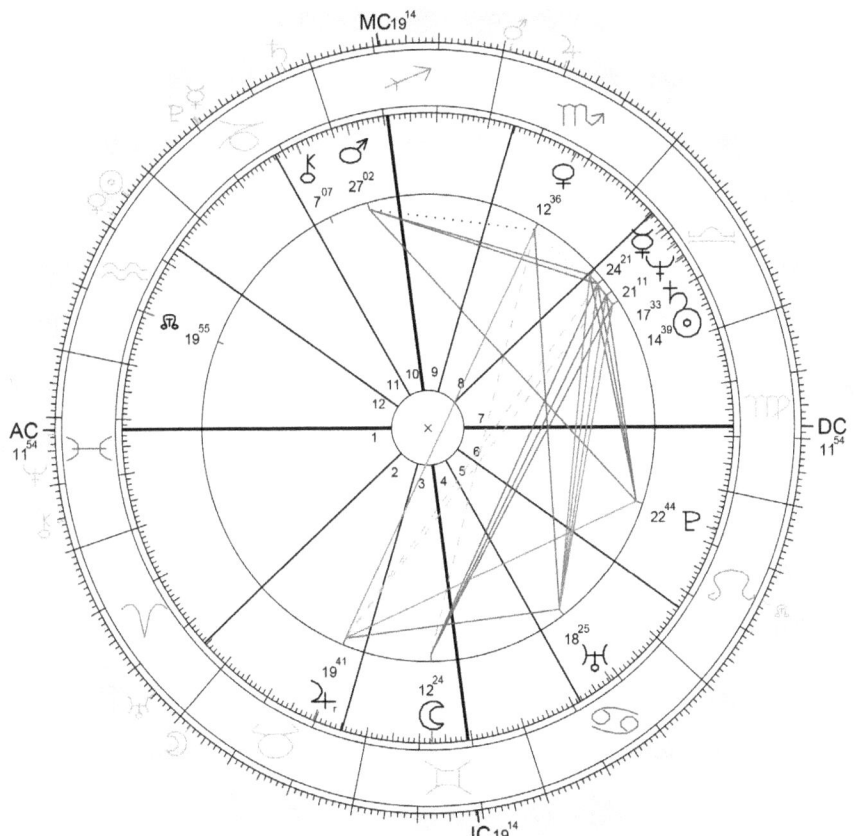

the infirmed and aged. Plus, it reminds us of things deeply buried that need to come to the surface and be cleared, once and for all, through service to others. Dan has the ability to clear payments due from past karma by self-initiated channels of service. By working with those limited and afflicted, he fulfills a karmic cycle originated in his lack of commitment for his brother and mother when he was Rick. Dan's profession in the medical industry does just that for him. He works for the aged and indigent in his work every day.

Only through service to others, will he free himself from the burden of this past life we saw, and possibly other past lives we didn't see. As Bob, he was already beginning this accomplishment. Bob was a loving and caring father and husband in Oregon. He gave his life to teaching his children to be self-sufficient and to appreciate the simple things of life. And what I know of Dan today, he is still performing those same duties and skills with his sons. He was involved in raising them at various times in their lives as well as still striving to be involved in their lives today in any way possible. Having a North Node in Aquarius, as Dan does, tells us that the there is an understanding of the unity of all life. A soul being in science, medicine, research or educational fields would be using the understanding of groups needs, rather than individuals, as an Aquarian would do.

With his South Node in the sixth house of day-to-day work environment and one's health, and with Leo as its ruler, we know many things about where Dan's soul most recently came from in his past lives. In the past his concern has been for himself (Rick). In this life helping others achieve a new and happier outlook is the way for Dan to find fulfillment and peace of mind. Leo is an optimistic sign and a fixed sign as well.

He will be a loyal leader in the workplace, and will always be there for his staff and peers. His past may have included not looking at his health. This had dire consequences as he passed at a younger ages as both Rick and Bob. Today, being in the health care industry, he is on top of his health. Many lessons have been learned in the two past lives as Rick and Bob.

The most obvious indicator of Dan's soul path in this life is to glance at the gathering of planets in specific houses. He has many important planets in his seventh house. By conjunction of his Sun with his Saturn, along with Mercury and Neptune very close by and all in the seventh house of partnerships, we know that partnerships and relationships of all kinds are important in this present life. Those same planets trine his Moon and sextile his Uranus in other parts of his chart as well. This aspect tell us that Dan's soul came to focus on being a caring communicator with original ideas when it comes to his loved ones and his associates at work. His soul wants to experience relationships that are loving and caring and long-lasting.

Now we are going to do some psychic card readings for Dan to see if they can illuminate any more details about his soul's path today. In the card spread, I tell Dan that he is beginning to enjoy life more, even though he is determined to complete his responsibility to work. I know that he is turning sixty-five this year, and he plans on retiring when he turns sixty-six and collect social security. He also hopes to continue to work part time as a purchasing manager, if his company will agree.

I tell Dan that he wants his joy and happiness to start NOW in reading the final card in the Celtic cross spread as the ten of Cups. The ten of Cups means being with people you love and trust and experiencing love. He sees himself doing lots of fun activities in the receiving of the seven of Cups, which means being involved in several activities at once and enjoying it. He and I had just been to a birthday party for his son in Colorado Springs the week before this reading, and we were looking forward to going to a concert the coming weekend at Fiddler's Green in Denver. These are activities that he had been too busy to attend when he was raising his two sons.

Next, I see the Knight of Swords in the area of the spread describing what is all around Dan. This card describes to us that he will be, (I was reading for the fall months of 2017 through the end of the year), making lots of changes in his life. Changes he wants to make are to play more in his free time, to spend more time with our new dog, Toby, a Rhodesian Ridgeback, and to plan more get-aways in his free time. Many plans are already in motion to achieve these goals. The cards are just confirming all that we know. I keep seeing the Queen of Wands being shown all around Dan. This card describes a multi-tasking woman who thinks outside the box and has an entrepreneurial spirit. I believe that would be me entering into all these new changes with Dan.

I also see the nine of Swords for Dan. He is pulling back from his work responsibilities, as he focuses on his family. These feelings would be reminders of Bob's life in Oregon. He worked hard, but Bob always found time to spend with his family. I know from this present life that Dan left Corporate America in higher management to work for Non-Profits years ago. This was a decision based on the need to be closer to his former wife and son that he never regretted.

We ask about the beginning of 2018 in the next card spread. I get the Ace of Wands which means new creative start for Dan in his life. He begins the year with an attitude that things are going to be changing for him in 2018. I see the ten of Pentacles which always refers to home and the security it brings. Dan is looking forward to not having to go into an office every day. This is something he has done for over forty years.

But I am also getting the ten of Swords for him. This Tarot card for me always represents the closing of a door of someone's past. It usually means they will never go back to that part of their life or relationship. The card indicates a finality "in the person's mind." Repeatedly in the spreads, I get the six of Cups for Dan. The interpretation of this card means to play and have fun. It is a new message to his self that is running through his mind all the time.

I asked of the cards if Dan would be receiving good news about working part time for his present company when he retires. The cards I received were the Justice card which means he is getting his "due reward" for working all these many years in health care. I also received the Strength card for Dan. This card means he will be approaching his request to go part time with strength and courage for what he thinks is a good opportunity for his company to use him at a reduced rate.

Remembering Rick and his life, we remember a man that did not come from strength. He did not even try to contact his Mother while he was in prison to let her know that he was there. Dan did not want to repeat this life of Rick's. That was a life of underachievement. In this life as Dan, he has worked hard to earn a good record of achievement.

Finally, the Knight of Wands appeared about his new job in the future that he would be working part time. This card represents creative thinking, but most importantly it usually describes a person taking on a new role or profession. The cards are saying to Dan that he will be accomplishing all that he desires in his future.

In summary, the three modalities of his past life regression, astrology natal chart, and psychic card reading, all concur about Dan's soul path in his present life. He is here to overcome his guilt of Rick's life, and be a dependable responsible businessman, father, and husband or partner. He is also here to receive love and happiness in abundance from his family and life.

Chapter Seven

Priscilla Daniel
The Healer Among Us

Priscilla and her husband, Mike, and their four daughters were in my first book, and were the subjects of a complete chapter, "A Family of Light Beings from Urabitzia." We discovered several lives where the entire family, all six of them, had participated in spiritually healing lives as teachers and healers. She also had an important life as a Native American woman married to a White man. They made herbal potions and gave healings to others much like the contemporary healing modality, Reiki.

The two of them, Priscilla and Mike, also had an important life in Egypt around 970 B.C. They were there to spread the light to humans and raise their vibration. They worked as embalmers when people passed over. Priscilla and Mike learned to wrap the dead bodies and seal them with herbs. Their hidden and true purpose was to help the deceased cross over into the spirit realm. Her guides told her that the entire family had come from Urabitzia. Her guides told her that Urabitzia is in our galaxy. And that her family had come to help with the ascension of human souls, and to spread the light to as many souls on Earth as they could.

This chapter focuses on Priscilla while Mike is the focus of the following chapter. The couple raised their children in Denver, and they still maintain their home in the urban area of the city. They recently moved to Grand Junction on the Western slope of Colorado to be closer to Mike's work. Her girls are all adults now, and one lives near her in Grand Junction, and the others are back in the Denver area.

Priscilla now feels it time to get back into her healing abilities, and to work with others to raise their vibration. Her guides have told her she needs to connect with herbs again, and use her Reiki skills for the benefit of others.

When we begin our session, Priscilla tells me that she has been experiencing some seizures and fainting spells recently, and wants to know how to help alleviate them.

She also feels she is starting a new path for herself in Grand Junction, and would like more input from her guides on how to go about opening her spirituality up to the light inside her.

As we begin the regression, she sees that she is outside and she is feeling faint and nauseous. She can feel her back twitching. Priscilla says she has the feeling that she broke her back. (She does tell me that in her present life, she had an accident riding a horse in Colorado Springs, and developed a compression fracture from it.) In this past life scene, she tells me she feels very isolated and weak.

She tells me she is wearing a rose print long dress with black heels. She has long auburn-brown hair, and she is in her 20s. When I ask her where she is and what year is it, she replies that it is the Mid-West in Nebraska, and the year is 1790. Priscilla says her name is May Beth.

In the next scene, she sees herself sitting at a vanity. She has a bonnet on, and she sees big curls draping over her shoulders. She is still in this small western town. She sees herself with horses now, and the horses are connected to a carriage. She says "I am not in the carriage. I am walking by myself, and I get trampled by the carriage and eight horses." Priscilla tells me that the runaway carriage and horses kill her!

As I ask her to lift her soul's essence from May Beth's crumpled body, and float up above her, she looks back down at the young woman lying in the cobblestone street dying. As she tragically leaves this life, I ask her to connect with her higher self, and ask what her soul's path was in that life as May Beth. Why did it end so early in her journey as May Beth?

From her altered state within the regression, Priscilla says that it was to experience the accident. Priscilla needed to know what it feels like to be suddenly killed by an accident. Sometimes our souls sacrifice a life of learning to learn from one big experience. Priscilla said that in her present life as Priscilla, she has always felt that she was going to die very young. This must be a carry-over from her life as May Beth. When we die suddenly, our soul is rather shocked with the sudden shift. Many times that trauma stays with us for many lives. Her higher self is taking this opportunity to revisit the trauma to release that life, and let her soul move on from it today.

Priscilla feels that May Beth was super intelligent for that time. The intelligence boosted her energy. She was very strong and independent. She had moved to that town in Nebraska by herself. That was very unusual, at that time, for women to travel or live alone. The soul of May Beth, (which is the soul of Priscilla), was totally fine with leaving that life so soon. Priscilla tells me that she had another life she needed to begin, and needed to leave May Beth's situation. She chose to leave through the accident to grow from that experience. Priscilla's soul is not as traumatized as another soul might be from this because she had chosen it an accident as a portal of departure from that life.

Other clients have told me the same thing. They choose to end a life early because they need to start a new life with members of their soul group in another life situation.

Souls do not look at leaving a life as humans do. Souls never die. They just have human experiences. May Beth may have felt she just didn't fit in in that western life in the small town for a woman of that time period. She put an end to a life that might not have accomplished much in order to move to a life with many of her soul group where her relationships could be more meaningful.

As we move to Priscilla's second life, Priscilla sees that she is outside on a cobblestone street. She says "I am in Ireland in the year 979. She is female, and she is wearing a long dress. Priscilla tells me that she has long, blonde hair, and she is about 36 or 37 years old. And she tells me her name is "Anna."

As she continues to walk, Anna sees a house up ahead. It is a very luxurious home. As she goes inside, she sees dark, rich woods throughout the house in the furniture, and walls with heavy, coarse fabric for drapes. It is her home, she tells me. Priscilla knows that she is married, and has a husband. Priscilla doesn't immediately recognize the soul essence of the husband, but later she says that he is, indeed, the soul essence of Mike, her husband today. Her children, she knows immediately to be the soul essence of her two daughters, Sarah and Jorden, today.

Next, Anna goes to the kitchen. She sees that it is more like what we would consider in contemporary times as a laboratory. Herbs are everywhere. She begins to mix a potion to be used as a medicine for a client. Priscilla says she lives her life as an herbalist for the community. Anna is extremely happy. She loves what she does. Priscilla says that Anna is loved and supported by her family. There is lots of love in their family. Anna feels very supported by her husband in her work, Priscilla says.

As Anna ages, she sees herself outside gathering herbs. Anna is just happy with all parts of her life. She know that she is about to have grandbabies in her life as Anna. She is going to have a big family. Priscilla's guides show her lavender. She says that they are telling her that she needs to grow lavender today in Grand Junction for her healing work. They go on to tell her that she could make soap from the local supplies. She can add lavender to the soap, but she could also take the local goat's milk and the locally produced honey, and infuse the honey and milk with lavender to make the soap. Her guides suggest she could bring in the scent of almond to add to this.

Priscilla moves to the last day of her life as Anna now. She sees that Anna is in bed, and she is now very old. She is tired and ready to leave this body. She passes peacefully. Her soul says goodbye to her family, and she sees that the soul essence of Mike gives her a hug as she pulls away from the body in bed.

I asked Priscilla to ask her higher self what her soul's purpose in that life was, and what she had wanted to accomplish. She said that it was simply to be happy. She wanted a simple life, to enjoy her family, her children, and enjoy the passion she had for helping others. She clearly accomplished that goal. I also believe that they showed her this wonderful life, even though it was over a thousand years ago, to remind her that she could have that same wonderful life today. It is a different time, but the same souls are in her life today. Priscilla is told she may have the love and enjoyment she desires in her present life, just as she did in this past life in Ireland.

It is also important to note that when we are shown a past life where we had specific skills; it is being shown to give us confidence to use those skills in our current life, if we feel the call to do so. Priscilla wanted to return to her spiritual roots, now that her family had grown to adulthood, and living lives of their own. Her higher self and her guides were showing her that it was all possible. She had all the experience she needed. As she delves back into herbs and growing lavender, she will recall all the experience she has from past lives. It won't be like she has to study a great deal to do this, her subconscious mind will recall her knowledge of this skill and will bring it into her conscious mind today.

Priscilla's guides come through now. She feels and sees that she has Archangels Raphael and Michael as her guides. We had met them in the previous regression and between lives regression work we've done together. They were not strangers to her. She recognized them immediately. They did not show her their wings, she said, but they were very stately looking and appeared to be in their 50s, both of them. She also felt and saw that Merlin was floating around her as well.

We asked her guides about the seizures. Priscilla was told that she was receiving bursts of energy to gear her body up for this new awakening to spiritual healing, and the amplification of energy caused the seizures and fainting. The Archangels said that by June it would all be normalized in her body, and she would no longer feel any discomfort. They wanted to get her attention by raising her vibration, and the side effect were the seizures, they said.

The Archangels and Merlin go on to tell Priscilla that this was all a plan for this present life. She always will have Mike and her daughters around her because they are part of her path. Mike is always going to encourage her to use her skills to help others in advancing their own light.

I performed an attachment release on the early death trauma of May Beth's life with healing Christ Consciousness light energy. We asked afterward if that had helped Priscilla with any repercussions she had had with her back in this life. They said yes, it did help. The Archangels also told her that she should take turmeric and magnesium for her body to fully recover from the light being sent to her body.

Priscilla went on to say that her guides were showing her that Jorden, her daughter, would be part of the business she would be starting in Grand Junction. They showed her tent gatherings, and healings being performed by her. She says they are getting her ready. They are starting to send her huge beams of light that come directly from her home planet of Uribitzia.

This was such exciting news for Priscilla. We then moved on to the Astrological Natal Chart for her to see any other personality traits she had brought through in this life to aid her in revitalizing a spiritual, teaching path.

As you can see in the attached Natal Astrology Chart for Priscilla Daniel, there are some strong planets in very important houses.

Priscilla has a Virgo Sun with her Moon in Aquarius. Her rising sign is Sagittarius. This "skeleton" describes a hard-

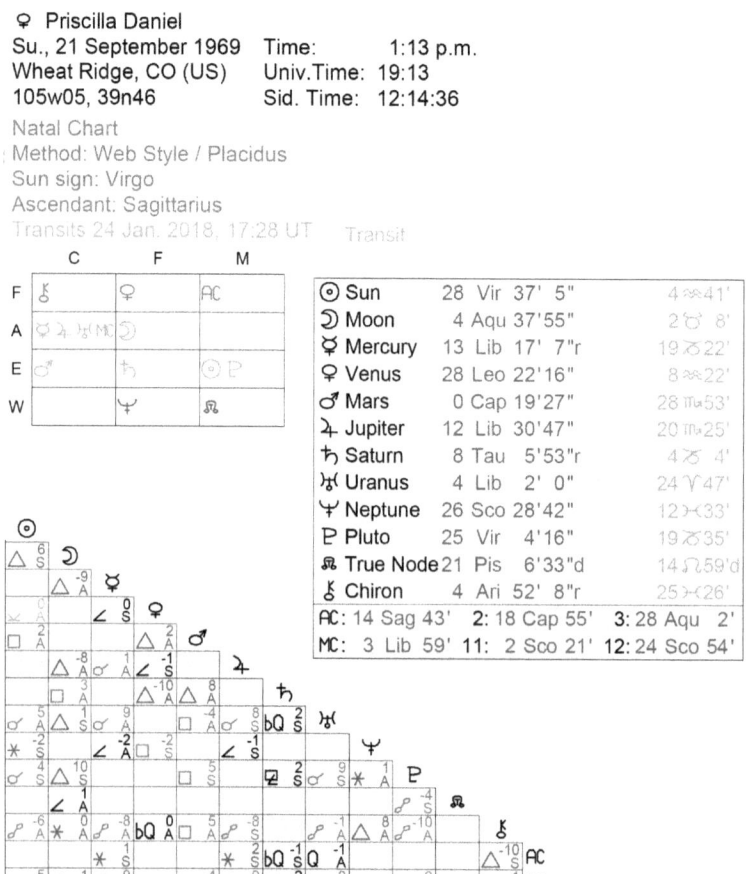

CHAPTER 7 - PRISCILLA DANIEL   123

working perfectionist, (she has a master's in technology skills). Virgos are always hardest on themselves. She expects nothing but the best from herself always. The moon in Aquarius describes a woman with vision for how the world could be for souls who live here. Aquarians always see subjects from a higher view. They are a fixed sign, so her emotional nature is to be a home provider for her children and husband. Her challenge is to never let them down, but be a creative achiever. This is a hard task she put before herself in this life. Her Sagittarius rising or ascendant would give her a pleasing, positive and

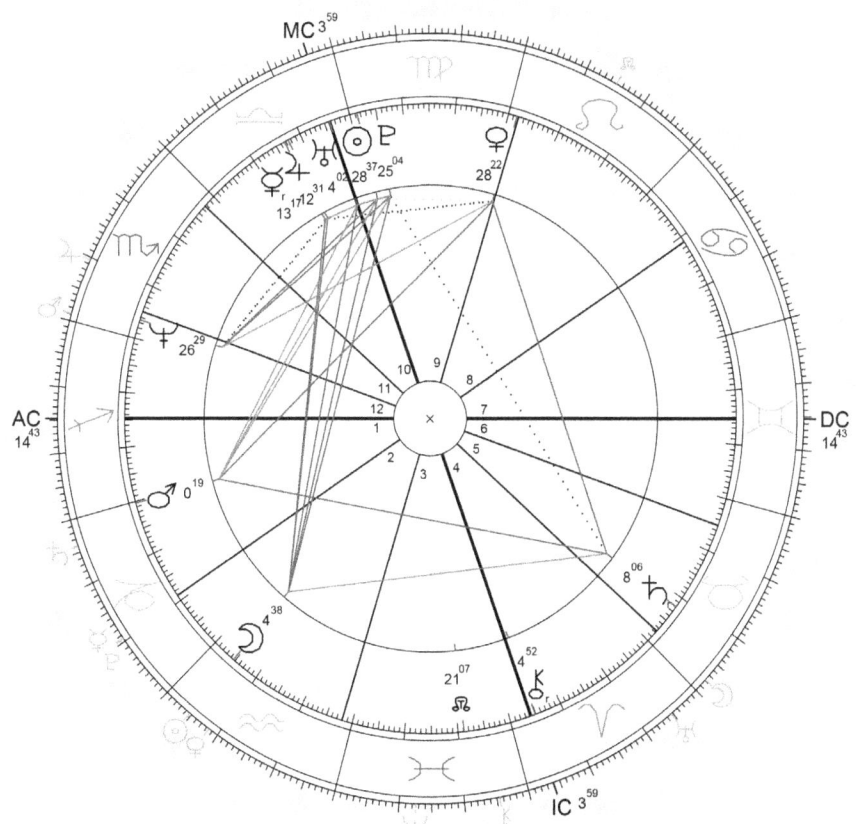

upbeat nature to the outside world. Priscilla always has a smile for you, and a positive message to give you.

As we look at the indicators for her most recent past life, we go to the placement of Saturn in her chart. Her Saturn is in the fifth house, and it is ruled by Taurus. Taurus is a fixed, earth sign. And Saturn being in this house of creativity, romance and children makes Priscilla a sure footed person. In her previous life, she more than likely was a free spirit who used her spirituality to help other people in a less professional mode. Having Saturn in Taurus would cause her to be an excellent teacher in more practical modes of spirituality.

For example, if she and her daughter, Jorden, began a soap and herbal business, that would be a practical way to express the use of healing. Even Astrology is a more practical way to help people understand their paths because it is backed by the science of the stars in the universe.

The ruler of Saturn is Capricorn. In Priscilla's chart, it rules her second house of money and goals. In this present life, she came to make a difference in her family's life financially in very ambitious ways. Priscilla has been involved in all of the remodeling of their Denver home. She contracted out the work to turn it into a classical home to rent out to singles and college students. As Mike works to provide, Priscilla has also learned to provide financially through the rental fees she establishes in her home.

Looking at Priscilla's Aquarius Moon in her second house would have Priscilla expressing her emotions and caring through the successes she can have out of her home renovations. The second house is where we express our values and how we go about being financially secure. Priscilla would be very attached to the success of the home renovations she oversaw. Even her spiritual classes on her land and out of her home in Grand Junction would be totally heartfelt. She would put her best effort into the teaching because her moon is guiding her success.

It could have been that she traveled a great deal and did not focus on family in her most previous past life. Priscilla, in her present life, now wants to change that, and put more emphasis on the home and family. That is why she was shown the life as Anna. As Anna, she had all the love and family very close to her all her life. But she was also able to have a very successful herbal and healing business out of her home property, as well.

Her guides showed her that she is ready to return to that type of achievement in her present life. Chiron is in her fourth house. The fourth house represents our home environment and inward personality. It is ruled by Aries in the fourth house. Aries, being a fire sign and the first sign of the Zodiac, is a near opposite to Chiron in this house. Chiron is an asteroid that has very powerful energy that promotes the challenge to discover our "wounded healer" caused from past life experiences and process it. Priscilla, as a soul, has had many lives where she was a risk taker in her healing lives. For example, she had been a guider of souls that crossed over in her Egyptian life that we saw. In this life, by having Chiron here, she is learning patience. She is learning to be there for her family and the home front before she leaps into the deep crevice of teaching.

Priscilla will master the challenge she came to achieve when she overcomes the fear of moving forward into this new path of teaching and healing after a grounded life of being mother, wife, and daughter for so many years up to the present. Wherever Chiron presents itself, we must push forward and grow to evolve our soul at those tasks.

Another indicator of most recent past life and her current path is the North and South Nodes. North and South Nodes are not actually material objects of the Moon. They are energy points in the atmosphere around the Moon that give us definite information about what our soul's path has been in our most previous life, which we find in the sign and placement of the South Node, and what we are currently working on in the present life to advance our soul, which we find in the sign and placement of the North Node.

Priscilla's North Node is in Aquarius which rules her third house of communication. Again, Aquarius is a fixed air sign, and Priscilla would be perfect as a teacher of higher consciousness by having her communication house ruled by Aquarius. Aquarius energy is comfortable in the higher dimensions. Also, she would have the vocabulary to speak on a higher dimensional level because she has her Sun and Venus in the ninth house of higher consciousness and education. Your Sun works as your ego and shows your passion. Your Venus is how you use your attraction of personality to connect to others.

Her South Node would then be in the opposite ninth house of higher learning, travel and spirituality or higher consciousness as well. Priscilla's most recent life was one where her focus was on being a free spirit that delved into the higher dimensions of the soul and spirituality, but was not so grounded or centered with family. Many times when we lose out on the groundedness of human existence, we as souls, crave to return to that comfort of love and giving that only family can give us. That is what Priscilla clearly stepped into in her present life. Her grown children and her parents are still very close to her in her present life.

In addition to the past life indicators, Priscilla has several important planets in her tenth house of career. First, she has Uranus placed in her tenth house ruled by Libra. That tells us that Priscilla will always have an unusual career path. Being ruled by Libra which is a hardworking and industrious sign, she could easily be a workaholic. She might never know when to stop if the work needs to get done. But, having Uranus there she is comfortable with unusual paths like her one of remodeling the family home in Denver. While Mike works out of state, Priscilla makes all the money and material decisions for them. This is her chance to show how she can contribute to the family financial success. She is determined to do a good job, however unusual it is for a woman to do this by herself.

In addition to Uranus, Mercury and Jupiter are also in the tenth house. Mercury is our communication planet. Therefore, it would be no surprise that Priscilla received a Master's in technology. Technology is the communication method of our future. Priscilla now has another mode of communicating to the public in her new career. She would be successful at webinars and informative websites that she designed herself. This is another example of unusual skills to the public by having Uranus in her tenth house.

The Jupiter placement just gives added energy and luck to anything Priscilla would do that would enhance her originality in her ventures into spiritual teaching and healing.

Her Moon is trining all these planets in her ninth and tenth houses. A trine is an aspect that complements the energy it trines. Being the Moon, this energy would emotionally support all her efforts to further her goals, associations and career paths in her life. Priscilla's heart gets involved in all that she does to help others. Her excitement comes from an inner knowing that she can truly guide others to see their own light and talent.

In conclusion, Priscilla came into this life to be grounded before she struck out onto her spiritual path. I met her just when the door was opening to her next chapter. I see a strong woman who is sure of herself through experience, yet lacked confidence to move forward on her spiritual path. Her higher-self wanted to make sure her home life with her husband and her daughters was clearly established. She wanted the loving relationships between them to develop and thrive before she delved into the second calling. Now it's time!

We moved next to the psychic card reading to help confirm what we had been told would be her future in Grand Junction. As I spread the cards into a Celtic cross, the King of Swords comes through with the Nine of Swords crossing it. Priscilla is thinking of Mike, (King of Swords), and knowing that he will fully support her in her new passion of facilitating women's groups and other endeavors. However, she moves forward thinking these ideas may be overwhelming for her, (Nine of Swords).

Other cards I flip over are the ten of Pentacles. It is adamant that she do all of these ventures through her home. The four of Wands repeats that Mike will support all her ideas and ventures as she moves through them. Next we get the Knight of Pentacles which means this is an idea she has repeatedly thought about. It's something she has always wanted to do in this life. Knight of Pentacles represents what we have always dreamed would make us the happiest.

She receives the three of Pentacles next in the spread. She realizes that people do not know her with these talents, but she knows she can do this. She has hidden these talents in the closet. It's time to "Come out of the Closet." Priscilla needs to turn to her friends, indicated by the next card I pull, the two of Cups, and connect with them to expand on her ideas and creative plans. They will help her get started into the healing classes she has been thinking about, or producing the soap bars with the materials she has access to locally. Her contacts will start her moving through the correct doors.

I then bring up to her a great book for her to read at this time, "Wishes Fulfilled," by Wayne Dyer. Wayne Dyer passed away in 2015 and wrote this book in 2012, one of his last books. I always say that he was my mentor, but he never knew it. I read so many of his books. He was master at taking a hard subject, and breaking it down for all of us to understand in layman's terms. In this book, he tells you how to teach your subconscious mind to follow through on a new challenge. That challenge can be a new career, a move, a new partnership, or even a new start-up business venture, such as Priscilla's. It is the book that taught me how to start traveling out of state to perform past life regressions. He states that your subconscious mind does not know reality from what you tell it is reality. So, at night before you go to bed simply visualize your new life. See yourself teaching the group, see yourself arriving at the location of the event. See yourself making those calls to connect. Then go to sleep and "marinate" on these ideas. In the morning, your subconscious mind believes you are already performing as you imagined. You speak and act with so much confidence!

I also reminded Priscilla she has a very close connection to her spirit guides. She should be looking for signs they will be giving her on her new journey. They will point to the right doors to venture through. If she hears a phrase from a song, and then later that day see the same phrase on a book title or in an article she reads, that is her guides giving her a message. If she smells something fabulous, then sees objects that remind her of that wonderful smell, then that is a message, as well. Her guides are telling Priscilla that she should be using some form of that item in one of her lotions or soaps.

In the next spread, we ask how her immediate future looked. The three of Swords came through. This card can mean many things, but for her it meant to spend time alone. Mediate on what you want for your future, the cards are telling Priscilla. She will reap a great deal from spending time alone. I saw the two of Cups for her. This tells me her daughters, Sarah and Jorden, and she will be working together in some capacity in this new path. The Joker came through next, and it says that she possesses many talents, and that when she least expects it, something will fall in her lap to move her forward on her path in the very near future.

The eight of Cups comes up next. It is to tell her to put behind her old responsibilities, they no longer serve her, and look out the horizon at the new path she is being offered. She should take it all in slowly. Finally, in the result position, we receive the Death card for her. This card describes total transformation, and it is going to be the result of the near future. My spreads usually go out four to six months from the present. By the end of 2017, Priscilla should be seeing a new life unfold before her.

In the next spread, we ask specifically about a heavy butter body cream she wanted to make from lavender, goat's milk, and honey. She also wants to start a meeting of women that she could facilitate. It would be a group of women that have goals they each want to achieve. She would help them find the answers to manifest their goals.

Again, we get the ten of Cups, which means she will be doing this at home and around her family, Mike, Jorden, and Sarah. The Hierophant and the Magician cards came through next. They tell Priscilla that she has all the knowledge inside of her to do this. She just needs to go within and formulate how she wants to begin. The Hierophant card tells us that we have talents, but only through contemplation will we know how best to use these talents. The Magician card says we have all the talent we need within us already.

At the close of the reading, the result card was the Crumbling Tower. For many, receiving that card scares them. They are afraid that all around them in their life is going to change for the worse and all will be very different. Many times the Crumbling Tower means something totally different. It means for Priscilla, all her daily habits, her actions, and her connections to others are going to be changing in big ways. But it does not mean in a disastrous way. The card means that her life will not look as it did previously in ever so many ways. Her life of solitude in Grand Junction is about to change into a mentor arena. Based upon the Result card, the Crumbling Tower, Priscilla will coach many and create a productive force that is not yet evident at the time of this writing. This is a change that she embraces and is very excited to see happen.

As I complete this chapter on Priscilla Daniel, I received an email from one of her best friends in Grand Junction who I have performed two past life regressions with. Lou Ann said she is so excited. Priscilla has just begun a women's group, and Lou Ann is so glad to be part of it! Looks like Priscilla is listening to the guidance of her spirit guides and is taking the first step into her new career path.

Chapter Eight

Mike Daniel

The Family Man

Mike Daniel is a Manager at an oil well facility based out of Grand Junction, Colorado. Most of his work has been in Utah, but he relocates often because of the nature of his work. He may stay at the job for a continuation of several weeks before he is able to come home for a visit with his wife, Priscilla, on their 35 acre home-site and log cabin home outside of Grand Junction in Mesa, Colorado. They have one biological daughter, who is 18, and two daughters from Priscilla's first marriage, plus a daughter from Mike's first marriage. However, Mike treats all his daughters the same. The young women are all adults with lives of their own and not living at home.

You have just finished reading about Priscilla's transformation and how she is about to start a new path. Mike seems to be on his own new path of transformation, but in a very different form. To learn about Mike's path, you must read about his past life sessions. They tell us much more about Mike than you would gather when you meet him.

I knew very little about Mike when I asked him to participate in my book. However, from the sessions I had experienced with Priscilla in the first book, I knew that he, Priscilla, and their daughters, plus her parents were all souls from another planet. Therefore, I felt he would be a good contributor to the book. I always learn from my clients through their experiences and their guides.

As we start the session, Mike had kindly taken his valuable time off to make the trip to Denver to do the past life regression session. We had decided that the Astrology Natal Chart and the Reading would be completed at another time over the phone or Skyping over the internet.

In the first scene, as Mike relaxed into his session, he saw that he was in a cave with a pool of water close by. He saw that there was an opening to the outside above his head. There were trees and vines coming out from the walls. When I asked him what he was wearing, Mike told me he was barefoot, barelegged and that he only had a short cloth wrapped around the middle of his body. He was bare-chested. He further told me he was a man in his 20s.

I asked him where he was, and he told me he was in South America and the year was 1752. He could not tell me his name. I asked him how he was feeling. "I am thirsty and tired, he said." He saw that as the young man, he started drinking the water from the pond in the cave.

The next scene had Mike as the young man on a beach, and he was about the same age. He was fishing and looking at the water. He caught a fish by using a stick. Next, I asked Mike where he goes, and he says that he sees the man following a trail into the bush. Then, I ask him, "What does the young man do next?" Mike says he sees nothing in his mind.

Over the years of doing sessions, I have had this statement told to me several times. It almost always means something comes to an end for that soul in that life. I went back to Mike, and said that your guides brought you to this life for us to discover something for you today. So, let's go back to the beach, and start the scene over very slowly and just take me step by step as the man moves into the bush.

"He is looking for firewood", Mike says. "He has with him the fish and he wants to cook it to eat." Next he sees that he is in a muddy place. It begins to rain. The young man sees a ledge of black rock. He gets up on the ledge. He is trying to get around the ledge, but the rain is making the ledge very slippery. Mike then tells me the young man is trying to hold onto the ledge, but it is so slippery from the rain that he is losing his grip. He drops his fish, and holds on with both hands, Mike says. Then Mike sees that the young man climbs down below him to find a way off the ledge and to keep from slipping. The man finds a hole there and just lies down.

Mike tells me the young man feels so tired and hungry. The water in the hole feels cool to him. Being in South America, it is very hot and humid for him. He feels weak and tired, Mike keeps saying. Next, the man starts to crawl. He realizes the rocks behind him are too rough to climb over to get down the rock, and the ledge above him is too hard to reach now that he has fallen down into the hole. It's getting dark for the man. Mike says the young man is tired, and he is going to sleep. The young man simply does not wake up.

As we realize the young passed simply from exhaustion and hunger, I asked Mike to pull his soul's essence out of the body and rise above the scene. When I ask if there is anyone in that life that he would like to put closure to and say his goodbyes, Mike says there is no one. That is very unusual. Usually there is a friend, loved one, or even an animal a soul wants to say goodbye to.

Then I asked Mike to continue to rise about the scene. As he leaves that life, I asked Mike to connect to his higher-self to discover his soul's plan or purpose coming into that life. We all come in with a plan that we are working on as a soul for our continuous growth.

Mike heard, "Independence." He told me that the young man simply walked away from his village at fourteen. His family didn't believe he would do such a thing and not come back. That is why it was so easy for him to leave. He never came back. He had been gone for over six years living on his own in the jungle. Next, Mike heard that the lesson he had learned from that independent life was that you need your family.

It strikes me that Mike is more integrated than appears on the surface between his higher-self and his human, ego self because he can say in the regression, "you need family." Sometimes our souls need to be reminded where we came from, and where we are today to appreciate what we have.

As we enter Mike's second life, he sees that it is nighttime, and he is walking on a cobblestone street. He sees lights in the buildings, but they are flickering, so he knows they are candles. Mike says he can see his breath, and that he is wearing heavy clothing that weighs him down. I asked him to describe what he has on. Mike says he is wearing boots, and pants and a coat that are made of wool. He tells me he is wearing a hat as well that comes down to his neck. Mike says he also has a full beard, and that he is carrying a sword as well. When I asked what his name and age are, Mike answers that his name is John, and he is thirty-five years old. Mike says John is in Ireland in 1435.

The next scene is of John going to the bar. There are people laughing, and there is a big, roaring fireplace. He is there to see his girl, Cheryl, Mike tells me. She is a barmaid at the bar. Mike told me that he did not recognize the soul's essence of the barmaid as anyone he knows in his current life today. They begin to talk, and Cheryl takes John's hand in the bar. Mike can sense that it has been a long time since Cheryl has seen him. He senses that because he sees that John is a shipmate on a ship that has been out to sea for a long time. This is his career, and he is gone for long periods of time at sea.

Mike senses that Cheryl has missed John terribly. She begins to feed him dinner with her fingers. She wants to feel close to John, Mike says. John and Cheryl love each other, he tells me. Cheryl does not want me (John) to go again on the ship.

We now move quickly to a garden. Mike tells me that John is forty-five years old now. He and Cheryl had a son that is now five years old. A few years prior, Cheryl had suddenly passed away from an illness that he could not save her from. John was broken hearted, Mike tells me, but he had no choice, but to raise the boy alone. Mike recognizes the son as the soul essence of his daughter, Aspen, today.

Mike goes on to tell me that John has become a blacksmith so that he could stay at home to raise his son instead of returning to the sea. John misses Cheryl, but he spends a great deal of time with his son. John becomes very busy as a blacksmith, and he teaches his son the trade as well.

Suddenly, Mike sees that there is a war, (It is during the Middle Ages in Europe,) and the community wants John to go with the soldiers. He is needed to make armor and swords. However, Mike sees that John insists on staying home where his shop and tools are. Mike tells me it is a long war, and that John's son joins him in the blacksmith business.

When I asked Mike if John ever remarries, he says no. And therefore, I asked Mike to move us to the very last day of John's life in this past life in Ireland. He sees John in his bed, and sees his son there with his new wife. They have a new baby. John is in his 70s. Mike feels John has had a full life, except for losing Cheryl. Between his son and his work, he was happy and fulfilled, Mike says.

I asked Mike is there was anyone that John would like to say goodbye to in putting closure to this life. Mike said that John would like to say goodbye to Cheryl. As the soul essence of Cheryl came through, John's soul thanks Cheryl for being in his life. She says that she wishes she could have stayed longer. I asked Mike to explore why she left so soon. Mike said that John was planning to go to sea again. Cheryl told John that by her leaving early, he would be forced to stay and raise their son. That had been their soul's contract. John had wanted to understand being closer to his child, and circumstances forced him to do just that.

Once again, I ask for the soul essence of John to pull away from that life. As he was rising higher and higher, I asked Mike to connect with his higher-self to discover his soul's purpose for that life in Ireland.

He told me it was to learn to be a father, and the plan had been for Cheryl to leave early so he would have to learn that role, whether he chose it or not.

We next asked that Mike's Master Guide come through and tell us more about what he just experienced. He saw a feminine energy. Mike told me she was large and wearing a white dress to her knees. She had short hair, and was in her forties. Her name was Sandy.

Interestingly, she told Mike that she had only been his Master Guide in the life in Ireland. When I asked about the previous past life in South America, she told him it was not important to know if he had any guides helping him in that life. We did not meet any other guides. I find when that happens, the Master Guide has chosen to be the spokesman for the session. Most people have anywhere from eight to twelve guides, but they may not individually introduce themselves at once. It may take many years of working with someone's guides for the additional guides to come through and introduce themselves to the human they are working with in the present life.

Mike went on to tell me that Sandy was telling him to "be happy." She also told him to "be content," and "appreciate what he had."

She went on to say what his soul's path was in his present life today. She said his path is to complete what he starts in this life. "Follow through and don't walk away from responsibilities," Sandy said. She went on to say that he is doing just that in his life today. Sandy said that he had graduated from all those stressful lives to be rewarded with this one. She said to take in all the happiness and contentment that Mike has now in his life. He is being rewarded for working so hard for so many lives to reach this accomplishment today in his present life.

Mike and I met using Skype, a few weeks later, to discover the details of his Astrological Natal chart. Attached you will see by his chart that he is a Capricorn Sun with a Cancer Ascendant and a Libra Moon.

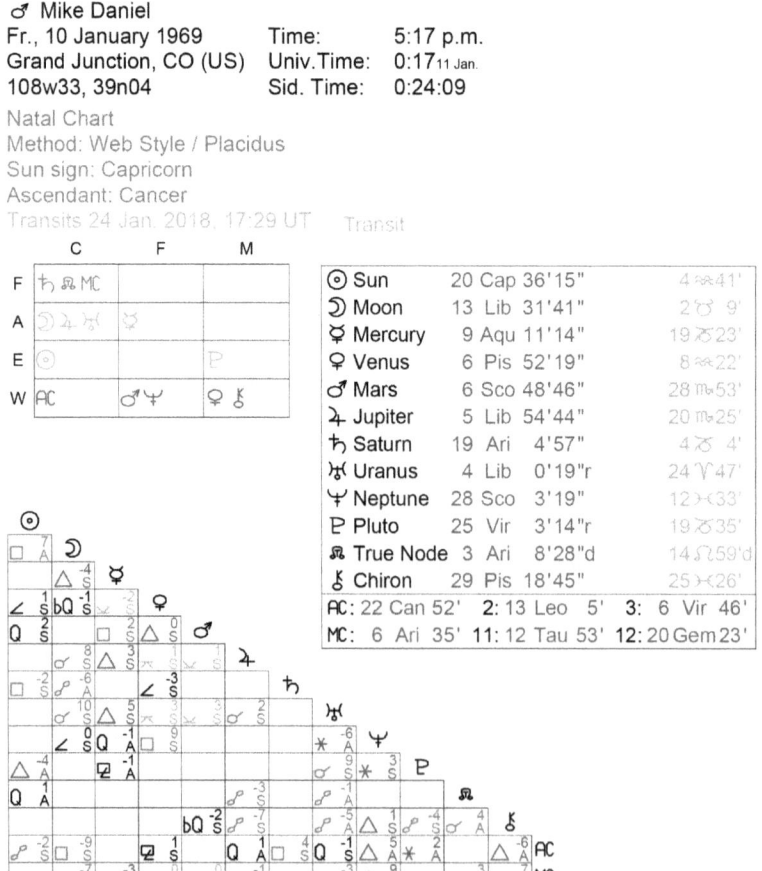

Capricorn is a Cardinal Earth Sun sign that describes a hard-working man who never gives up on a project. The Cardinal element tells us the he is a man of action. He is person who follows through on anything you give him. He has common sense, and is practical above all else. The Cancer Ascendant gives him an emotional quality to his work. His co-workers see a man who cares about their welfare. He might even be nicknamed the "Mother" because of his caretaking skills on the job. He worries about his staff just like a mother hen. He also is a responsible husband and father.

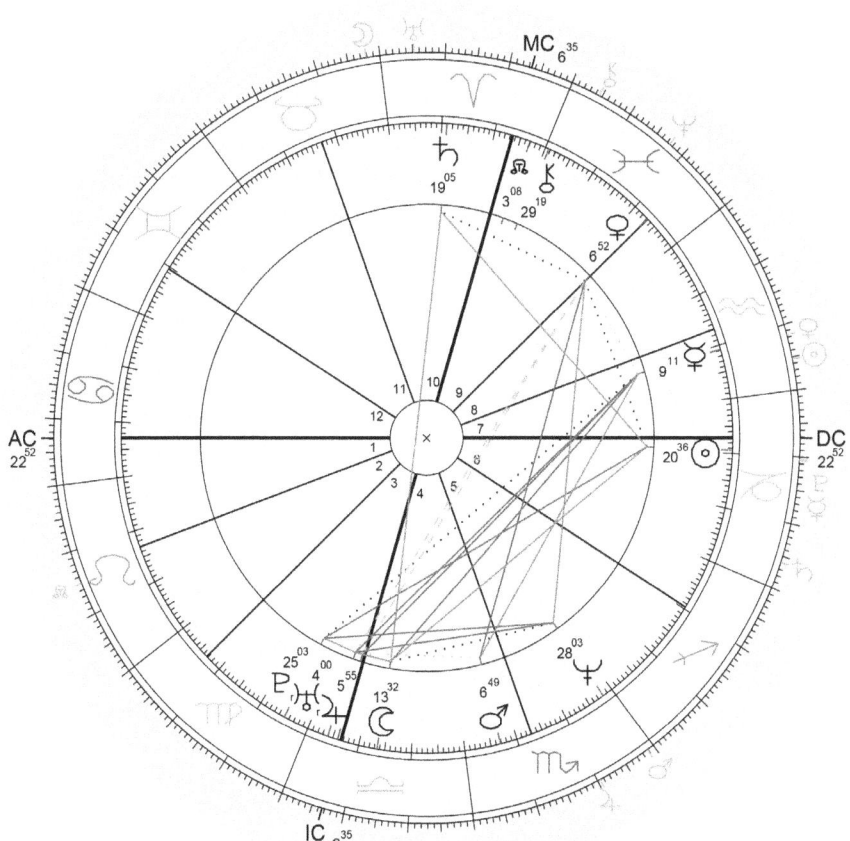

Mike's Cancer Ascendant is a Water sign and gives him the psychic intuitiveness to easily read other people's feelings and emotions. It is one of his traits that helps him in business immensely.

His Libra Moon would make him romantic in nature as well as dependable as a partner. Libra Moons are masculine in nature and also a Cardinal sign. They like to take action and solve problems. Mike's Libra Moon makes him intelligent with tender reactions to his family's moods. He is also steely underneath when a crisis hits them. He is the man to call when an emergency happens.

Mike's Sun is in his sixth house of work and health. His ego is reflected in the performance he gives at work. He redeems much happiness by excelling at work. The oil fields are a great place for Mike because he is able to express his full commitment to the job. Something that few people can do is to put in the long days it takes to get the job done in the fields. Mike can master that with no problem.

However, his heath may suffer at times. The sixth house is also the house of personal health. He would probably admit that many times he will finish his day at work, and do nothing but get ready for the next one. Mike could look at his body and the rest it needs, more in the future.

In contrast, his Libra Moon is in his fourth house of home. Home is very important to Mike. His family back at home is the center of his life. He is loyal and determined to be strong for his family with Libra as his Moon sign.

Now, after describing Mike's "Skeleton", let's move to some indicators of his most recent past life, and his current life path to see if it overlaps with what the past life regressions implied for him.

One of the first indicators is Saturn in the tenth house of public career. Mike's soul chose to come into this astrological chart with Saturn in his tenth house of career. He very well may have been more self-centered in his most recent past life. He may have not focused on his career, and moving forward in his success in the outside world. He may have even used people for his rise to success in whatever he was involved in. In this present life, he wants to change that as a soul path. Because Saturn is ruled by Aries in his tenth house, which is a Cardinal Fire sign, he is active with a take-charge personality, and a feeling that he must give back in service in whatever endeavor he pursues. His most recent business, before the oil fields, was his own excavation business using heavy equipment. These two professions are both roles where he must give back in service to his clients and to his staff in order to be successful at his job.

His Saturn also opposes his Moon. This makes his Saturn a little weaker and a little more insecure. This could be caused by a poor relationship to his Mother or a distant Father. His soul asked for this because he has been a little too confident in his most recent past life. We ask for these lessons to bring our soul back to center.

Another indicator is where the ruler of Saturn is in his chart. Capricorn rules his seventh house of partnerships. He came into this life to be very stable and dependable in his relationships, whether it be his marriage partner, his work partner, or friends that he made in his life. He shows he cares by what he does for his partnerships. For example, he bought his wife, Priscilla, a car, slightly used, when he wanted to thank her for keeping the home fires burning while he was away working. In his most recent past life, he may have been more about his own priorities than anyone else's.

Mike's Chiron is placed in his ninth house of spirituality, higher learning and travel. His ninth house is ruled by Pisces in his chart. Pisces is the most spiritual sign of all the signs who can intuitively read the feeling of others. I know that Mike's soul has lived many lives helping to raise the consciousness of others around him as I learned from he and Priscilla's past lives from previous sessions with Priscilla.

He, also, was raising his own consciousness when he volunteered to be a single father, and grow very close to his son in his past life in Ireland. To learn to connect on a deep, loving level is something that many fathers and sons never get to experience because of work responsibilities, and our busy lives today. He wanted to make it his entire life's path as John, and asked that his dear wife leave early for him to do so. That is an advanced soul that will do that for the human experience and understanding. The path of Chiron in this ninth house is one he has carried for many lives. It is to help to raise the consciousness of all who are around him to understand the concept of oneness. It is a fact that we affect each other in all that we do. The pain that one experiences, we all experience. I believe in our current state of affairs in America, we see this, when a terrorist or single rebel kills innocent people such as in Orlando or Las Vegas. We all feel the pain and the loss.

Even the young boy in South America, in Mike's first past life, was shown how loneliness and sadness of being without one's family can cause a soul to give up and leave his life. It's just too hard to make it in this world without someone to care for you.

Next, I looked at the North and South Nodes in Mike's chart to understand his most recent past life, and his current goals in this present life. His most recent past life, as indicated by the South Node being in his third house, was a prominent life where he spoke and others listened. In his chart, we see the symbol for the North Node in his ninth house. The South Node is always the opposite house from the North node. In this case, that would be the third house. The third house rules communication, writing, and speaking of any kind. His ego was stroked in that past life. But, now his soul has returned to balance himself by giving back in service to others.

Mike is still speaking and people are listening, but by having his North Node in his ninth house, he is doing his speaking in a teaching way to help others. He is mentoring his men under him to understand the bigger mysteries of life in his present life. One of Mike's job responsibilities is to train the men under him to follow in his footsteps, and he does this with heartfelt sincerity. His slightly insecure feeling of being a teacher is caused by Saturn and its aspect to his Moon in the tenth house. This aspect causes Mike to be very humble in teaching others of his higher consciousness ideas.

Mike definitely came to teach in his present life. It is indicated by the aspects of several important planets in his third house of communication. Jupiter, Uranus and Pluto all trine Mercury in his seventh house of partnerships in his chart. This tells us that the boost of luck that Jupiter brings is given to him when he talks or teaches. Uranus tells us that he will talk or speak outside the boundaries of what people expect of him. And Pluto tells us that he has a quiet strength in telling his stories that needs to rise to the surface for Mike. This will return him to his roots of being a teacher with confidence. In the sessions with Priscilla for my first book, he did this several times as her partner. Even John was a teacher to his son. He was so good at it that his son went on to take over his business.

Mike and I met later several days later, using Skype, to do his psychic intuitive reading using Tarot cards. As I ask what is in store for Mike in the immediate future, I pulled the Hermit card. This card expresses that one has talents that they need to go within and access, and bring them back to the surface to be used in an appropriate way. When I asked Mike about this, he explained that he is being told at work that he has the opportunity to step into a higher position called "Directional Drilling Supervisor." This position would give him the power to manage the actual start-up of a new drilling installation. That new information explained the pulling of the next card which was the eight of Cups. This card expresses the energy of Mike wanting to put his old position behind him, and start focusing on this new path of the future which is now being presented to him.

He told me he is not confident he fully understands the entire job description for this new supervisory position, yet he wants it very badly. The next card I see is the Temperance card. This card expresses that he will have to be patient, and not lose hope that he can master this new challenge. Just keep on keeping on, it says. At the end of the spread, I received the Knight of Swords for Mike. This energy means a lot of changes are happening all around him in the near future which will require him to make many important decisions about his path.

This result of the cards thrilled Mike. He is very eager to take on this new position, even though he doesn't fully understand it at this time. In the next spread, I asked about the future coming up for him in the next few months, and received totally different cards. The Crumbling Tower is always a card of great change. People fear this card, but actually it can be a blessing if you are wanting change. It means that everything around Mike, that he takes for granted in his life, is about to change. His daily patterns, his schedule, and work associates are about to change. Next, I see the three of Pentacles for him. This means that talents that have laid dormant in his personality are about to be pulled out and used for the first time. A new job would bring new skills.

Then I go on to see the Lovers card and the eight of Wands. Lovers card can indicate that he will be developing new, close relationships demanded of this new job opportunity. The eight of Wands means that at first it will be sluggish while he learns, but eventually the position will take off for Mike and move forward. Finally, I received the Justice card and the Ace of Pentacles. These cards mean that he will receive his promotion. The Justice card means he will receive his due reward because he has earned it, and the Ace of Pentacles means he will be making more money as the result of it. The Ace of Pentacles almost always means a new path and more financial success.

I now moved to a short spread of five cards to determine the time table for Mike of this new life shift. I saw that in October and November of 2017 he is working on both positions. The two of Swords, which I pulled as the center of the question, explains that he is torn between two positions at the same time. I also see that all of this is requiring a lot of hard work on Mike's part. This is expressed by the four of Pentacles which means to focus on work, and do not take any risking detours.

Finally, I saw in the last Celtic cross spread for the new year of 2018 that the time was here for Mike. He was to begin his full mentoring position to these men. This teaching would be required in this new position. I had pulled the Empress card which expresses that the time is "pregnant" now. The time is here and can no longer wait. He has fully transitioned to the new role after months of training and holding down both positions. It is now October as I write this so we will see if all works out, timing wise, as the cards predict.

I also received the Sun card and the nine of Cups card. These express that Mike has been waiting for this mentoring and leadership role for a long time. The Sun card is the most positive card of 78 cards in the deck. It means all your life's ambitions are before you. The nine of Cups expresses "what one has been hoping for has arrived".

I have to mention that I kept receiving the three of Swords in the spreads. This card would be referring to Priscilla missing Mike a great deal over these several months. Hopefully, this will remind Mike to go home as often as he can while he is transitioning to this new position for the company.

I would definitely say that the Astrology Natal chart tells us that Mike's soul came prepared to do his teaching and mentoring in a humble way to people working right next to him. He is grounded by his Saturn influence in the tenth house of career for this new role.

He will be calling on all his important planets in the third house, Jupiter, Uranus, and Pluto, to inspire and teach the staff in the Directional Drilling Supervisor position.

The two past lives have prepared him for this role. The young boy's life showed his soul how important family is, and that he cannot come into a life and expect to be successful on his own. We all need others in our lives. The past life in Ireland for John showed his soul how important an influence he can have when he is dedicated to teaching and working for others. His profession, as a Blacksmith, helped many soldiers have the tools they needed to go off to battle. His mentoring to his son showed how he made a difference in the boy's life because it gave him a skill he could be proud of and help him the rest of his life to provide for himself and his family.

Mike is having a reward life of successes in family and work after many challenging past lives. He has learned how to open his heart to his family and fellow workers.

Epilogue

What is Next for These Souls?

All of my clients including myself and Dan are looking for the same thing. We seek to complete what we came into this lifetime to achieve as a soul. We feel compelled to grow and strengthen our abilities to engage with this challenging planet.

I believe past life regression hypnotherapy sessions can help every single individual on earth. We learn more about ourselves as a soul and what experiences we have had and how we grew as we processed through our past lives. Many times clients leave with so much more confidence in themselves knowing that they have battled prejudice against the color of their skin, or their economic class, or even their gender.

We, as a world of humans, are here by choice to help mature and grow this beautiful planet. Our history of wars and battles, and presently our actions against our environment, be it the waters we drink or the air we breathe, is affecting our futures as well as this planet's for years and years to come.

As we realize that we are the souls of the grandchildren coming back in future lives to live in the environment we are creating currently with our car fuels, our animal-for-food carbon monoxide off gases, and even the run off of toxins from fertilizers into our fresh water, our souls can come back from these past life regression sessions with a new determination to make changes.

If we can feel and experience in our past life regression sessions what our souls have experienced by being all nationalities, all races, and both genders many, many times, then maybe we can begin to drop our prejudices and realize that we are all ONE. What one of us does affects us all.

Martha Staffer understands why she is so fearful of our present politics and the election of a new President because it reminds her soul of the uncertainty she experienced in the Nazi ruled days in World War II. This feeling in her soul makes her very conscious of not being judgmental with her circle of friends and her work associates.

Or Dan Ely, who brings his forgiveness to others in his current life situations, transforms a past life consciousness of retribution where he killed a man in revenge for the death of a brother. In this life, Dan is open to helping the indigent and disadvantaged. His soul remembers how he felt to neglect his family and be imprisoned. In his current life, Dan is ready to lend a hand without a filter of prejudice and be of service whenever called upon.

If we can truly know through regression sessions, and astrological natal charts, and psychic card readings what our soul's path is for our present life, we can accomplish so much more through this clarity and not squander this very precious time we have here on Earth.

Love and light to you all, Lee

Astrology 101

To understand the chapter information on the Astrology Charts, it might help to know the basic information of a chart and what all the symbols mean.

1) There are twelve signs in the zodiac.

Aries – March 21st to April 21st
Traits are leadership and strength. They charge forth to butt their heads against any obstruction in their way. Their sign is the Ram. They make good executives, have original ideas and are full of energy.

Taurus – April 22nd to May 22nd
They are slow, steady and stubborn. They cannot be pushed. They are the sign of the bull. It takes time for them to adjust to a new idea. It takes a great deal to anger a Taurus. Possessions and material things are of great significance to those born in Taurus.

Gemini – May 22nd to June 22nd
They have the sign of the twins. It represents the dual forces, the opposition of the human and the divine in all of us. Gemini is called the butterfly of the zodiac for it flirts from situation to situation to gain growth through experiences.

Cancer - June 22nd to July 22nd
Cancer people are passive, receptive and emotional in nature. Cancer is the mothering, sustaining, nurturing sign of the zodiac. It is symbolized by the crab. It carries its house on its back, and retreats into it when threatened by exterior forces.

Leo – July 22nd to August 22nd
Leo people have great courage. It is the most vital of signs and has tremendous energy. Leos have a confidence and an assurance around all who they meet. Leos have loyalty to those who they love. They are very attached to those they love.

Virgo – August 22nd to September 22nd
The symbol of Virgo is the Virgin, holding a sheaf of wheat. Just as the Virgo people collect, digest and correlate facts for the mental values, the virgin denotes purity and perfection. Virgos desire to reach the highest possible perfection in life.

Libra – September 22nd to October 22nd
It is the union or marriage sign of the zodiac. The soul has become the "we" consciousness. The development of relationships is the most important attainment for the Libran. Many lawyers fall under this sun sign.

Scorpio – October 22nd to November 22nd
Scorpio is the mystery sign of the zodiac. Scorpios have a very strong reserve and are not easily known. Much lies hidden

below the surface. They command respect. The Scorpio tongue can sting just as a scorpion.

Sagittarius – November 22nd to December 22nd
The sign is represented by the centaur (half human and half animal). Most are friendly, outgoing, optimistic, and extroverted. "Don't fence me in" is their motto. They love to travel and in later years turn inward and upward.

Capricorn – December 22nd to January 22nd
Their symbol is the mountain goat. It climbs toward heights, solitary and alone. Nothing will stop them achieving success. They are capable of great strength. They possess leadership, patience, persistence and practicality.

Aquarius – January 22nd to February 22nd
Aquarians are forward thinking individuals who live in the future, not in the past. Aquarians are much more emotionally involved in their work than they are with people. They are rebels and individualists and do well in big business.

Pisces – February 22nd to March 21st
Their symbol is one of two fish. One fish represents the personality and one represents the soul. Pisces is the most sensitive sign of the zodiac. They are moody and introspective. Yet, they are capable of great achievements.

2) There are ten planets and one asteroid in the zodiac.

Sun - It represents our will, our individuality and our spirit

Moon – It represents our personality and our emotional nature

Mercury – It represents our mind, and its link between spirit and matter

Venus – It represents our personal affections and appreciation

Mars – It represents our energy, initiative, and courage

Jupiter – It represents the principle of expansion wherever it appears

Saturn – It represents the principle of contraction wherever it appears

Uranus – It represents independence and originality in all matters

Neptune – It represents compassion, chaos or cosmos in all things

Pluto – It represents regeneration, coercion, or cooperation

Chiron – It represents the wounded healer in all of us

3) The signs fall into different forces:

<u>Cardinal signs are action signs and are fast and direct:</u>

Aries, Cancer, Libra, and Capricorn are Cardinal signs.

<u>Fixed signs are consistent and persistent in all they do:</u>

Taurus, Leo, Scorpio and Aquarius are Fixed signs.

<u>Mutable signs are pliable and adaptable to circumstances:</u>

Gemini, Virgo, Sagittarius, and Pisces are Mutable signs.

4) There are four elements known as Fire, Air, Water and Earth in which the signs are divided:

<u>Fire signs are energetic and enthusiastic. They include the signs:</u>

Aries, Leo, and Sagittarius

<u>Air signs are mentally astute and deal with relationships. They include the signs:</u>

Gemini, Libra, and Aquarius

<u>Water signs are reflective, responsive and emotional. They include the signs:</u>

Cancer, Scorpio and Pisces

<u>Earth signs are physical, practical, and grounded. They include the signs:</u>

Taurus, Virgo, and Capricorn

5) There are twelve houses in the zodiac.

First house: What you look like and the personal self.

Second house: What you own and your view of money and material possessions.

Third house: What you think and all things to deal with communications, including social media and the internet.

Fourth house: Your home environment, real estate, domestic affairs.

Fifth house: Rules romance, children, and creativity.

Sixth house: House of day to day work and personal health.

Seventh house: All relationships: personal, family, and business

Eight house: House of other people's money, regeneration & sex.

Ninth house: The realm of superconscious mind, long journeys, and expansion of the mind through education.

Tenth house: Prestige, honor and one's standing in society, career.

Eleventh house: Goals and objectives, friendships and groups, hopes and ambitions.

Twelfth house: The house of that which is hidden. It rules hospitals and institutions. It is the house of serving or suffering.

6) Aspects between the planets. Aspects are lines of force between the centers of energy (planets) in the magnetic field of the individual.

Conjunction: Planets that are 0-10 degrees apart. Give one strength and power from the two planets energy.

Opposition: Planets in one's chart that are 180 degrees apart. It is a tug of war between the two planets to grow the strength of the individual and make them stronger

Square: Planets that are 90 degrees apart in the chart. It creates obstacles in the personality that must be overcome.

Trine: Planets that are 120 degrees apart. This aspect creates harmony and union between the two energies in the individual.

Sextile: Planets that are 60 degrees apart. This aspect give an opportunity or fortune to the individual.

Tarot Cards 101

The deck of Tarot Cards consist of 78 cards, of which twenty-two are known as the major arcana. The remaining fifty-six are referred to as the minor arcana.

The minor arcana is then broken down into four different suits---wands, cups, swords, and pentacles. Each suit contains an ace through a ten, followed by a Page, Knight, Queen, and King (known as court cards). Each of the suites represents one of the four elements:

Wands---Fire
Cups-----Water
Swords—Air
Pentacles—Earth

The cards contain archetypal images, pictures, and symbols that make a connection with one's subconscious mind. The major arcana focuses on the higher matters of life, while the minor arcana indicates situations in our daily existence. But both are important. Think of the major arcana as the bricks and the minor as the mortar that fills the spaces, holding it all together.

I only use the Gilded Tarot created by Ciro Marchetti and published by Llewellyn. I believe they are the most visually stunning Tarot cards available. But, there are many, many different artists' conception of the 78 cards and they basically mean the same influences for the reader.

The fours elements are shown in four important colors:

Minor Arcana
Wands=Red=Fire
Cups=Gold=Water
Swords=Blue=Air
Pentacles=Green=Earth

All the Major Arcana cards have a black border color key on their borders to match each suite of the lower arcana.

There are many spreads that are popular with readers. Know that a single card does not a spread make. The cards will tell you more detail the more cards you work with. I like the "Celtic Cross" which consists of 10 cards laid out in a square effect with two cards crossing each other in the middle. I pull an extra four cards to express the client's thoughts in more detail, and I pull three or four around the end result to give more details to the final result of the spread.

In ending, I want to give you a simple breakdown of the meaning of the cards so you can refer to them as you read the chapters and perhaps it will intrigue to get a deck yourself. They always tell the truth, even if we do not want to hear it.

MINOR ARCANA

SUIT	WANDS	CUPS
Element	*Fire*	*Water*
Ace	New Venture of life	Love and relationship
Two	Initial accomplishments	Important union, balance
Three	Completion of first stage	Happiness, joy, love
Four	Stability, marriage plans	Don't let this opportunity pass
Five	Conflict, quarrelling	Feelings of disappointment
Six	Success, achievement	Happiness from the past, play
Seven	Defending position	Lots and lots of choices
Eight	Fast progress after delays	Abandoning a path, unfulfilled
Nine	Perseverance, final push	All your wishes are coming true
Ten	Feeling overburdened	Committed, marriage card
Page	Good news, work related	Happy emotional news

MINOR ARCANA

SUIT	WANDS	CUPS
Element	*Fire*	*Water*
Knight	Change of home, work	Love proposals
Queen	Warm cheerful woman	Kind, sensitive woman
King	Entrepreneurial, dynamic	Warm, thoughtful man

MINOR ARCANA

SUIT	SWORDS	PENTACLES
Element	*Air*	*Earth*
Ace	Triumph over adversity	Start of successful venture
Two	Stalemate, indecisive	Maintaining balance in life
Three	Quarreling, apart	Success through effort
Four	Rest and recovery	Overly cautious, fear of loss
Five	Deceit, unfair dealings	Temporary hardship, loss
Six	Harmony after strain, journey	Successful gains, gift
Seven	Diplomacy, not going as planned	Work and patience rewarded
Eight	Feeling restricted by fear	New job, long term project

MINOR ARCANA

SUIT	SWORDS	PENTACLES
Element	*Air*	*Earth*
Nine	Sense of anxiety, despair	Financial success and security
Ten	Disappointment, end of cycle	Financial stability, money assets
Page	Delayed news, slowness	Good news financially
Knight	Fast decisions, serious man	Positive outcome, reliable man
Queen	Perceptive lady, efficient	Woman of words, capable
King	Men in uniform, strong	Man who works in finance, property

MAJOR ARCANA

NO.	TITLE	MEANING
0	The Fool	Unexpected Opportunity, choices
I	The Magician	You have all the skills to succeed
II	The High Priestess	Intuition, unexplored potential
III	The Empress	The time is NOW, pregnant times

MAJOR ARCANA

NO.	TITLE	MEANING
IV	The Emperor	Overly cautious, fear of loss
V	The Hierophant	Wise person, institutions, government
VI	The Lovers	Love partners, love choices
VII	The Chariot	Patience and perseverance
VIII	Strength	Strength through quiet determination
IX	The Hermit	Inner wisdom, contemplation
X	The Wheel of Fortune	Karmic change, a new cycle
XI	Justice	Getting your due reward, contracts
XII	The Hanged Man	Self-sacrafice, to be of service
XIII	Death	Transformation, major change
XIV	Temperance	Patience, balance, healing
XV	The Devil	Passion for another, indulgence

MAJOR ARCANA

NO.	TITLE	MEANING
XVI	The Tower	Destruction of all in your daily life
XVII	The Star	Optimism, all your hopes and dreams
XVIII	The Moon	Dreams, emotions, unseen depth
XIX	The Sun	Success, happiness, marriage
XX	Judgement	New beginning, renewal, rewards
XXI	The World	Triumph, achievement, happiness

About the Author

Lee Mitchell, Certified Past Life Regression Therapist, has been facilitating regressions since 2008. She also gives spiritual intuitive readings out of her home office and at Celebrations, **www.celebrationstore.com**, a Metaphysical Bookstore in Colorado Springs, Colorado. Astrological Natal Charts is also a passion for Lee. She lives in Denver, Colorado in the city of Highlands Ranch. Lee travels to California and Texas to do past life regressions and between lives sessions a couple of times a year, as well as sessions in Denver at Isis Books, **www.isisbooks.com**, and out of her personal home office. Lee and her life partner, Dan, have a furry son, Toby, at home with them. He is a Rhodesian Ridgeback hound they rescued from the Ridgeback Rescue Organization, **www.ridgebackrescue.org** in 2016. Lee Mitchell has authored two other books, "The Soul's Journey," and "The Divine River of Life."

You can reach Lee on her website, **www.crystalsoulpath.com** or by email: **lee@crystalsoulpath.com**.

www.ingramcontent.com/pod-product-compliance
Lightning Source LLC
Chambersburg PA
CBHW071713090426
42738CB00009B/1759